D0977148

"THIS
IS HOW
WE FLOW"

"THIS IS HOW WE FLOW"

RHYTHM IN
BLACK CULTURES

Edited by

ANGELA M. S. NELSON

University of South Carolina Press

© 1999 University of South Carolina

Published in Columbia, South Carolina, by the
University of South Carolina Press

Manufactured in the United States of America

03 02 01 00 99 5 4 3 2 1

Library of Congress Cataloging-in-Publication Data

This is how we flow : rhythm in Black cultures / edited by Angela M. S. Nelson.
  p. cm.
  Includes bibliographical references (p.) and index.

  ISBN 1-57003-190-8
  1. Afro-Americans. 2. Blacks. 3. Rhythm. 4. American literature—Afro-American
authors—History and criticism. 5. Afro-American aesthetics. 6. Aesthetics, Black.
7. Afro-American arts. 8. Arts, Black. I. Nelson, Angela M. S., 1964–
  E185 .T45 1999
  305.896'073—dc21   98-40207

Permission to reprint current copyrighted material quoted in this volume is gratefully acknowledged: Chapter 6 is from *The Preacher King: Martin Luther King, Jr. and the Word That Moved America* by Richard Lischer. Copyright © 1989, Oxford University Press, Inc. Used by permission of Oxford University Press, Inc. T. J. Anderson, *Variations on a Theme by M. B. Tolson.* Copyright © 1969 by T. J. Anderson. Extract reproduced by permission of T. J. Anderson. William C. Banfield, *Spiritual Songs for Tenor and Cello.* Extract reproduced by permission of William C. Banfield. "Can't Keep a Good Dread Down," "Dread Eyesight," "Dread John Counsel," and "Ganga Rock" by Benjamin Zephaniah. Copyright © 1985 by Benjamin Zephaniah. Extract reproduced by permission of Benjamin Zephaniah. "Come Into My House" by Dana Owens and Mark James. Copyright © 1989 by T-Boy Music Publishing, Inc./Queen Latifah Music/45 King Music. Used by permission. All rights reserved. "Harlem Dancer" by Claude McKay. Used by permission of The Archives of Claude McKay, Carl Cowl, Administrator. "Yoke the Joker" by V. Brown, A. Criss, and K. Gist. Copyright © 1991 by T-Boy Music Publishing, Inc./Naughty Music. Used by permission. All rights reserved.

CONTENTS

ILLUSTRATIONS

Music Excerpts

Map

ACKNOWLEDGMENTS

I would like to acknowledge and thank my former chairperson, Christopher D. Geist, and current chairperson, Marilyn F. Motz, of the Department of Popular Culture at Bowling Green State University, and the Bowling Green dean of the Graduate College, Lou I. Katzner, for their financial support of this project.

More importantly, this book could not have been completed without the assistance of my research fellow Lori L. Tomlinson. Lori is completing her doctoral dissertation in American culture studies. During the summer of 1995 and most of the 1995–96 academic year, she assisted me in preparing this manuscript as it was being compiled. Her skills in editing, which she acquired in large part while at the Bowling Green State University Popular Press, were invaluable to me. Without her work of high quality, *This Is How We Flow* would not have been completed as smoothly as it was. To Lori, I am most grateful.

In addition, I am especially indebted to my husband, Randolph, and my daughter, Israelle, for putting up with me and this process as best they could. I truly thank them for being "real." And, finally, I thank God for granting me peace of mind and for guiding my thoughts. "His praise shall continually be in my mouth."

"THIS
IS HOW
WE FLOW"

INTRODUCTION

ANGELA M. S. NELSON

> Many things contribute to the value base of African culture—priority of group identity (inherent in collective and communal participation) over individual identity; respect for elders who are closer to that which is divine or spiritual in the universe; acceptance of unseen forces as real, visible elements in the organization of ones own behavior. Respect for fertility and procreativeness as manifested in praise for generative powers. The ability to bring the vital spiritual force into being—all combine to create the fabric of African culture and frame African behavior under the commandership of vital rhythm.
>
> Alfred Toldson and Ivory Pasteur,
> "The Aesthetic Conceptualization of *Nzuri*."

> The relationship between Africans and rhythm is not only constant but it is essential. It is not a question of having rhythm or not having rhythm but how well does one negotiate rhythm in life and in the artistic expressions of life. On time or off time is a simplistic result of a very basic relationship with rhythm. The complexity of rhythm generates multi-layered, multi-leveled, multi-existence so that it is possible for people to respond to different layers, levels and planes and still be in harmony with the framework of the rhythms and with each other.
>
> Kariamu Welsh-Asante,
> "The Aesthetic Conceptualization of *Nzuri*."

> Rhythm is the architect of being, the inner dynamic that gives it form, the pure expression of the life force. Rhythm is the vibratory shock, the force which, through our senses, grips us at the root of our being.
>
> Leopold Senghor, cited in Zadia Ife,
> "The African Diasporan Ritual Mode."

Rhythm is *the* textural element that allows us to see and understand best African creative expression. The poet Leopold Senghor, first president of the republic of Senegal, states that rhythm is the "organizing force" that makes the black style.[1] Technically, rhythm refers to the organization of musical events or sounds and thus the flow of music in time. But Senghor's claim that rhythm is the "most perceptible and the least material thing"[2] better characterizes the "personality" of rhythm, for this "least material thing" is the chief organizer and energizer in the lives of human beings.

Although rhythm is an important concept in all forms of music, it holds a very unique position in traditional African thought. It is precisely the following of "rhythm" that attuned African cultures of old to the occurrences of natural phenomena like the rising of the sun, the flowing of rivers, and the beating of waves upon seashores. Because rhythm is concerned with temporal organization or duration, it is also connected to the concept of time. Sociologist John Horton says time is diverse. It is always social and subjective to the degree that human beings derive their sense of time from their experiences and their place in the social structure.[3] However, he continues, diversity of time is rarely tolerated socially because a dominant group establishes, conceptualizes, and objectifies its own time. Therefore, dominant groups view all other conceptions of time as subversive to their social order.[4]

The same observation made about time applies to rhythm. A group (any group of people) establishes, conceptualizes, and objectifies its own rhythm. All rhythms (other than the group's established rhythms) can be viewed as subversive to the group's social order. However, as a function of time, the complexity of the African and African American approaches to rhythm perception and production are largely due to the value placed on spontaneity and the communal nature of oral improvisation, plus the fact that rhythms communicate experience.[5] Sociologist Raymond Williams details how the arts are a means of sharing between human beings, putting an experience into communicable form. He believes rhythmic production is one good example:

> Rhythm is a way of transmitting a description of experience, in such a way that the experience is re-created in the person receiving it, not merely as an "abstraction" or an "emotion" but as a physical effect on the organism—on the blood, on the breathing, on the physical patterns of the brain. We use rhythm for many ordinary purposes, but the arts comprise highly developed and exceptionally powerful rhythmic means, by which the communication of experience is actually achieved. . . . [I]t is a physical experience as real as any other.[6]

Again, the nature of rhythm, as Williams alludes, lies within its "way of transmitting a description of experience." For African Americans, descriptions of transcendence, or what Victor Turner calls "communitas," a heightened form of community, are transmitted whether these descriptions be in dance, music, language, literature, or film.

In oral-based cultures, such as that of Africans and their American descendants, all oral communication is a reflection of the immediate environment and the way in which its members relate to that environment. Africans and African Americans use rhythm to reflect and relate to the larger environment. For instance, Molefi Asante says one reason enslaved Africans survived the ordeal of bondage, an environment out of their immediate control, is because they learned how to "work work." That is, enslaved Africans learned how to get "in time" with the rhythms of their labor. If the enslaved did not know how to "work work," explains Asante, then the work would work them—to death.[7] Slave labor was so cruel that Africans uniquely adapted rhythm in order to create spiritual and physical harmony in their chaotic lives.

The pervasiveness of rhythm in African American culture and music is so great that several scholars have commented on what it means to people of African descent, comments that are also replete with theological implications. Dona Richards' Afrocentric interpretation posits that rhythm is *ntu,* or the universal life force.[8] In other words, rhythm is the fundamental, spiritual organizer of the lives of African Americans. Or, according to Kariamu Welsh-Asante: "Rhythm is integral to the life force of every African. Rhythm is omnipresent."[9] It is an organizer that permeates all beings as well as African and African diasporan philosophical conceptions of the world in which Africans must be "in time" rather than "on time."[10]

Jon Michael Spencer's theomusicological interpretation of rhythm, in his article appropriately titled "Rhythm in Black Religion of the African Diaspora," argues that rhythm was the "theological imperative" of African religions.[11] In other words, the ultimacy of rhythm (being "in time") led Africans in diverse religions of the diaspora to dance, sing, and "shout" together. Rhythm, not the drum as mistakenly assumed by some antebellum whites, was the "essential African remnant" that secured and maintained the spiritual and physical harmony of enslaved Africans.[12] Furthermore, Spencer argues in his *Rhythms of Black Folk* that even though the diaspora generally "de-drummed" the enslaved Africans, it did not "de-rhythmize" them.[13] In addition, he says that the rhythms of black folk leave an "imprint on us," which is manifested as soul or what he prefers to call "rhythmic confidence." This phenomenon is realized when blacks return to sacred sources of Afro-rhythms very much in the way that religious blacks return to such sacred places as the black church to ponder "vital questions" and, basically, to get rejuvenated.[14]

In traditional African music, rhythm is used to achieve an integration of music and community.[15] Indeed, rhythm impels black people to come together. Zadia Ife reminds us that because the traditional African understood the holistic nature of rhythm, music was incorporated into the labor, rituals and various celebrations that the community engaged in."[16] While Ife finds little division between music and rhythm, it is important to note that rhythm is the motif that undergirds all black activity. To be sure, people of African descent use rhythm to articulate their moral, theological, and philosophical beliefs. Rhythm, the essential element in black music, philosophically communicates "religious" experience in African cultures and helps its ritual participants to reach "communitas."

While rhythm is generally acknowledged to be significant to black music (as noted above), as it is significant to all musics of the world, music is not the only black cultural product permeated and organized by rhythm. Quite the contrary, as Kariamu Welsh-Asante suggests, all black expressive products are guided by the principles of rhythm: "The relationship to rhythm is key not only in dance and music but in visual arts, architecture, theater, literature, and film."[17] This fact partially explains the purpose of this volume, which is to explore the meaning, motif, and theme of *rhythm* in diverse black cultural products.

All of the work in this book was undertaken by scholars trained in such mainstream disciplines as religion, literature, and political science as well as African, African American, and American Studies. *"This Is How We Flow"* begins with Juliette Bowles's poetic, scholarly discussion of rhythm in African American music. It is indeed appropriately placed because it is not only a discussion of black rhythm but is itself a rhythmic performance in writing similar to Albert Murray's classic book, *South to a Very Old Place* (1971). The chapter by musician, lecturer, and United Methodist minister Mark Sumner Harvey is an examination of rhythm in terms of its conceptualization in jazz music, and in William C. Banfield's chapter, written from the point of view of a composer, the author suggests a methodological framework for composing black music. He calls black rhythm the "Undeniable Groove." Angela M. S. Nelson, a professor of popular culture, discusses the primacy of rhythm in African American rap music of the eighties and nineties.

The motif of rhythm is also explored in black oratory, literature, and film. While Dr. Martin Luther King, Jr., has often been recognized for the rhythmic quality of his speeches, homiletics professor Richard Lischer illustrates this phenomenon in more detail here. Next, Ronald Dorris and Darren J. N. Middleton deal with two distinct genres of black literature in their chapters. Dorris elucidates on the motif of rhythm in one of Claude McKay's poems, "Harlem Dancer." Middleton examines the power of rhythm to move people to write and to act for social justice in the poetry of three Rastafarian dub poets.

In her chapter, D. Soyini Madison, a scholar of performance studies, discusses rhythm as ritual, modality, and discourse in the film *Daughters of the Dust*. While "having rhythm" gave African Americans opportunities to perform to a mass film audience in the thirties and forties, now, because of Madison's work, it can be said that the rhythms of black folk provide options for extracting meaning from black film of the eighties and nineties.

Rhythm as expressed in two countries of Africa are demonstrated in the last two chapters, by Alton B. Pollard III and Zeric Kay Smith. Religion professor Pollard provides a historical-critical survey of freedom songs in South Africa from the 1800s up through to the 1990s. Political scientist Zeric Smith's essay, while at the surface somewhat unlike the others in this volume, is perhaps the most insightful in that he demonstrates that "macro- and micro-rhythms" exist within the political context of Mali, thereby lending credence to scholars' claims that rhythm organizes and frames African behavior regardless of context.

In sum, the primary goal of *"This Is How We Flow"* is to illustrate the ways in which a commonly referred to musical element—rhythm—is in fact a central theme for and foundation of all African expressive products. A secondary goal is to suggest, by example, that an African aesthetic does indeed exist and that this aesthetic necessarily revolves around the motif of rhythm.

CHAPTER ONE

A RAP
ON RHYTHM

JULIETTE BOWLES

The evolution of forces and patterns giving rise to syncretic cultural forms such as jazz is not merely a mechanically occurring result of, for example, European musical styles and techniques being mastered and infused with African and African American elements by musicians such as Scott Joplin, King Oliver, Fletcher Henderson, Coleman Hawkins, Charlie Parker, and others whose innovations are then "quoted" and incorporated into the eclectic styles of other black and white composers, arrangers, and musicians. Rather, I believe that, being more than the sum of its parts, a cultural form (in this instance jazz) emerges holistically—the result of countless interactions between various kinds of human and environmental patterns and forces, significant among which are rhythmic patterns and forces.

> The great silence before the beginning.
> And then came time: the beginning.

In the beginning, there was the "Word," there was "om," there was the "big bang" and nada—rhythms vibrating into matter throughout space.[1] Rhythm is the fundamental expression of the fundamental energy. Atoms and molecules vibrate; the smallest particles of matter dissolve into undulating waves—energy pulsates. Planets revolve around axes in their routes around suns, generating the diurnal and circadian rhythms that give rise to plant and animal life. Consciousness radiates, hearts pump, lungs expand and contract, females ovulate in cycles that are related to phases of the moon, uterine contractions expel new life—rhythmic motions generate and sustain all of life. Leaving "time" in its wake, rhythm is the very dance of life.

Outside of a hut in an Akan village, a woman skillfully parts bristling hair springing from a girl's scalp and braids it into a rhythmic visual pattern—zigzagging intervals of smooth, glistening scalp outlining contrasting, triangular-shaped patches of dark, crisp hair. A stylized representation of the sankofa bird of Ghana whose crooked anatomy makes it appear to be looking backwards, the swastika-shaped hair design has a meaning: "Turn around and fetch your history."[2] Rhythmically geometric patterning runs all through the hair, textile, and sculptural designs of traditional West African cultures, forming a visual counterpart to the intense audile and kinetic rhythms that fundamentally structure these cultures.

Situated some 3,000 miles and some 300 miscegenated years away from the experience, I consult books and journals for meanings of the powerful, syncopated rhythms that pulsate through my being. Some answers are in the books; others are in the blood. Pondering the meanings of the rhythms of black hair: regular/suppressed/relaxed and irregular/animated/kinky, it seems obvious that zigzag parts and gravity-defying, unextended natural braids, twists, and tufts are what rival Goldilocks, not a sister's emulation of the Goldilocks ideal.

Uneven, asymmetrical rhythm is characteristic of the musical, dance, and material expressions that spring from the African American folkbase. According to this aesthetic, irregularity has more interesting and provocative qualities than does regularity (although extended, repetitious, regular rhythm is employed for another type of entrancing effect in the black folk idiom).

> *Like Lady Day say, she couldn't stand to sing a song straight let alone sing the same song the same way twice. And when Maceo took it along the broken off-beats between blasts from the James Brown Band all the way down to the bridge, won't it funky now?*

When free, the polymorphously spiraling hair of the Akan girl has a counterpart in the polykineses of her dance and the polymetry of the accompanying music. Rhythms of body structure, movement, and physiological processes combine in the production of, and continuously interact with, cultural structures and processes. Most fundamentally, as indicated by the findings of particle physics, rhythms are vibrating waves of information that give rise to forms perceived by the senses.

> Shake it all up. What meaning do it make?
> Shake it all up. What meaning do it make:
> St. Louis, Sony and *Soul Train,*
> "A Love Supreme" and Rupert Sheldrake?
> A theme about tuners, energized fields and blues
> about transmitters, transformers, transcendence and payin' dues,
> about spirit in and among systems.
> And also if blessed—and it can only be by grace:
> a rap on relations between rhythm and "race."

Biologist Rupert Sheldrake proposes a holistic explanation of learning, creativity, and evolution among animal species that has implications for the study of the cultural production of human beings. Laboratory tests have shown that animals who are not related to each other through direct genetic ancestry or social or physical contact learn specific tasks more quickly than previous generations of the species. Describing the process through which this evolution occurs as "morphic resonance," Sheldrake argues that the behavior of any given species in the past builds up and, through resonating fields, affects the behavior of the same species living later.[3] "A Love Supreme" was the expression of John Coltrane's comprehension of the ultimate unity of life, which is indicated by phenomena such as "morphic resonance."

In considering this thesis, one may surmise, for example, that not only through physical contact with other musicians but also through time-transcendent, all-pervasive fields of rhythmic electromagnetic energy, 'Trane was heir to the accumulated intelligence and technique of pioneering musicians who came before. Through his innovations, this intelligence and technique was encoded and made available to other musicians. How is it that jazz musicians can "play more notes" than their predecessors or that athletes run the one-minute mile at increasingly faster rates and perform ever more astonishing feats on the basketball court? The morphic resonance thesis is plausible because some aspects of human evolution occur more rapidly than theories of genetics and explanations of physical communication and practice can account for them.

Apart from this intriguing but debatable thesis, one thing is for sure: evolutionary cultural change in the United States is empowered and expedited by vast, interconnecting communications and transportation networks and technologies.

Southeast Georgia, 1958: A moonman from the marshes plugs his guitar into an outlet, conjuring ancient frequencies: the shrieks and hollers of shipholds and canefields. His final wail, strung out over ages, trailing the long whine of a Norfolk Southern locomotive. Symbols of high intensity, drive and speed, trains had vivid meanings for black people. Diesels ran all through the arrangements of Fletcher Henderson, Don Redman, Chick Webb, Billy Strayhorn and Duke Ellington—chariots north and west to freedom. Twentieth Century Unlimiteds cross the prairies, atoning in tempo for the white man's transgressions—appeasing the spirit of the land: "Cherokee," Charlie Barnett's passionate repentance carried forth by the heartland's Charlie Parker. Rolling over tracks laid by gangs hitting lines with strikes, grunts and rhymes: "Walk it on down the line, now, ha. Talk it to time, now, ha!"

Big band, small band chuggin' cross the land,
pumpin' hard, blowin' back,
laying formidable licks on the track.
Driving beats straight down on zigzagging rails of syncopation:
the quickest way to get to Harlem.
Back in slavery times, in heavenly songs and lullabies sweet:
airs melodic—half-measured, neat.
The other music was complex, percussive and free:
thigh-slapping smacks, grunts, thumps and stomping feet.
God almighty raw rhythm!

Rhythmic shouts and percussive beats combined to synchronize and empower hard, tedious labor, to ease protracted misery, to sanctify the ring shout from a shuffin' dance and dispatch its possessions deep into trance.

An infinitely bountiful resource in circumstances of extreme deprivation, the rhythm of black folk music had to be extraordinarily powerful to raise its makers from the most abject depths to the heights of ecstasy during moments of celebration and praise, and to sustain them on an ongoing basis, day to day.

> New Orleans, late 1920s
> Zora slipped through the red and white doors near the quay. The people were patting, tapping, slapping, stomping and chanting away. The music, an elaborate polyphonic discussion, worked the mighty magic of fractured percussion.

The next day, Zora opened her notebook and began to write:

> *The music consisted of chanting, clapping and stamping. The heel patting was a perfect drum rhythm. The hand-clapping had various stimulating breaks. The fury of the rhythm . . .*

She paused, wondering how to describe the rhythmic force driving the dancers until they became possessed.[4] The "stimulating" quality of rhythmic breaks apparently inspired enslaved black folks to call their dances "breakdowns." Once sound and movement was broken all the way down, people in bondage boundlessly soared.

The "down" condition was adroitly shaped into verbal concepts by practitioners such as Betty Jones, a former slave in Charlottesville, Virginia:

> Saturday nights we'd slip out the quarters an' go to the woods. Was an ol' cabin 'bout five miles 'way an' us would raise all de ruckus dere we wanted. Used to dance ol' Jenny *down*. Who was Jenny? 'Twon' nobody but me, I reckon.[5] (emphasis added)

"Jenny" could well be an articulation of a sensibility that is commonly supplied by Africans listening or dancing to percussive music—a sense that is an integral part of the music itself. This subjective, silent sense of timing (a "metronomic pulse") is strung out in beats that underscore and *complete* the audible beat.[6] To dance this sensibility down would mean that Betty Jones was not dancing to or with the clapping, chanting, and stomping (and perhaps fiddling or strumming) in the cabin; she entered the music as interpenetrating movement, weaving kinetic accents smoothly within and around percussive beats and roughly contradicting the beats with strokes of her body, the "contradictions" being "just for the funk of it," as her great, great grandchildren might well say.

The overall experience was not only polymetric but polymorphous: many converging and diverging kinetic elements interacting with many converging and diverging audible elements. In formulating style, black folk creators realized that differences (breaks) and inconsistencies (syncopation) can be more dramatic and thrilling than similarities (continuities, harmonies) in dance and musical expression.

Betty Jones created a further dimension of drama by setting a glass of water on her head: "The boys would bet on it as I danced. I had a big wreaf roun' my head an' a big ribbon bow on each side, an' didn't waste a drop of water on none of 'em."[7] The rigidity of the upper part of Betty Jones's body provided a counterpoint to the fluidity of the lower parts. Rigidity and fluidity are integral, rhythmic components of black dance movement. According to this aesthetic, anyone wildly flailing arms and legs "can't dance," no matter how rambunctious the accompanying music may be. A dancer's freely formed, multi-patterned movement finds its most skillful, gratifying, and dramatic expression within intervening and underlying controls of stasis.

Oases within intervals of stases: powerful absences, jagged reliefs, rhythmic displacements, stop-time—wellsprings of the transfixing mix. Curious visitors to praise houses spoke of "almost unearthly effects"— "invisible powers," emerging from lurching pulsations of this kind: an overmind. As breaks and wave-like fluctuations in tone, rhythm shows how the Void and the form are inseparably related.

Betty Jones gave up dancing when she became a Christian, but the *down* spirit survived in her praise of the Most Precious and is reflected in her speech: "Dem was de days when me, Jenny and de devil was runnin' in de depths of hell." Black folk dialect resounded with poetry: spunky rhythms accenting and punctuating highly figurative speech.

Sound and motion broke all the way down as Crow's crooked ol' Jim limped about a Louisville livery stable, singing a disjointed little rhyme, at the end of each verse, marking time: hopping high on wings of feeling, flying inside himself through the ceiling, landing on one foot and setting his heel a-reelin':

Wheel about, turn about
Do jis so,
An' ebery time I wheel about
I jump Jim Crow!

Spying the scene, Tom Rice fashions an act, paints himself black, and to the crowd's astonished delight, "Jumps Jim Crow" on stage that night. And the rest is much of the history of the American musical theater.

Rebuilt broken rhythm penetrates piano playing, is broken back down and built back up on the eighty-eight, producing "ragtime." "Doctors"—cutting masters—are the mothers of this rollicking new sound. In contests to cut out all competition, black pianists create ever more intricate renderings of the rhythms of modern times. Uprights throb with reverberations of port cities and frontier towns—rhythms of docks, brothels, saloons, stables, horse races, and world's fair midways, front parlors and back alleys, soda fountains, street cars, assembly lines, pounding machinery and flickering nickelodeons.

Informal yet virtuosic, ingenuous yet complicated, improvised yet calculated, mechanical yet syncopated, ragtime, the novelty music of the 1890s, is the
sound of the coming century.

"Yet" is "and": an aspect of relativity.

> Raggedy time on brass band marches, raggedy time in jooks, raggedy
> time in early twentieth-century physics: on Einstein's moving clocks and in
> Planck's sporadic spurts of quanta.

Within the most minute particles of matter is nothing but oscillating fields—
the organizing patterns of life. Rhythm is a form of intelligence. Perception occurs
through a rhythmic process—waves of sensory information from the environment interacting with information stored as wave patterns within the "mind."
Only wave patterns could hold all of the information we "know."

The tempos of modern, urban life in the United States filtered through the
antennae of the advance guard, and black musicians responded with a hotter and
even more prodigiously ragged music—"jass," which was amplified and conveyed to the masses through networks and fields of mechanical, electrical, and
magnetic currents. From the inside out and back again in continuous cybernetic
loops along crisscrossing networks of information-encoding neurons and synap-
tic bridges, out through proliferating national communications and transportation systems, popular forms of arts and entertainment contributed to a rapidly
evolving mass culture in early- to mid-twentieth-century America.

As multiple originating sources were consumed within the burgeoning mass
culture, interconnecting fields of influence evolved between an emergent youth
culture in the dominant society and the more marginal African American experience. The novel amusements, dances, competitions, and slang expressions that
fascinated young Americans in the 1900s were influenced by both authentic and
caricatured elements of black style. The first national dance fads, for example,
originated in sprightly fox and turkey trots that were introduced to style-setting,
young, white revelers in New York by black bandleader James Reese Europe.

In searching for ways to express the spirit of the modern during this period,
European visual artists found the disjunctures of African rhythms especially
appealing. Duchamps' disjointed yet flowing image of a woman descending a
staircase had a counterpart in the fragmented effluvium of ragtime and the
emerging jazz. The revolution in Western visual art revealed essences of the subjects portrayed—as did African sculpture. The Cubists' stylized abstractions and
broken picture planes captured and concretized the spirit of the subject in ways
not available through orderly photorealistic renderings. Again, the creator breaks
down subject matter to rebuild and reveal it in new ways.

As James Reese Europe, true to his prophetic name, introduced "le jazz hot"
to Europe during his service in France during World War I, dance halls where
the music was played were springing up all over back home. Popular pastimes of
listening to, learning to play, and dancing to syncopated music spurred the production of sheet music, piano rolls, gramophones, and upright pianos and

devolved into the formation of Tin Pan Alley. Engineering advances in the record-ing of sound and transmitting it over long distances met with a clamor for more, more, more of that thrilling "devil's music"—hot jazz and low-down, inebriating blues—begetting a recording industry that would soon rock the planet. African American improvisation and North American technological innovation produced new marvels of sound and style throughout the century.

In the twenties, mass popular cultures of black entertainment and "flaming youth" continued to evolve in complementary ways. In 1923, the "Charleston" gallivanted out of James P. Johnson's Broadway hit musical *Runnin' Wild* to become the dance rage of the decade. Johnson had composed the influential "Carolina Shout" a few years earlier. Duke Ellington recalled, "Everybody was try-ing to sound like "Carolina Shout" that Jimmy Johnson made on a piano roll."[8]

As black musicians made arduous, painstaking efforts to master technique at ever more demanding levels of virtuosity, Ellington learned "Carolina Shout" by passing his fingers back and forth along the mute yet eloquently textured sur-face of a piano roll, and James P. practiced playing piano through a sheet and in pitch darkness to refine his touch.[9] Nevertheless imagery of blacks as simple, carefree folk possessing natural gifts of rhythm prevailed in the coalescing "Jazz Age" culture—still, a mostly youth-oriented phenomenon. (Jazz would finally triumph as an intergenerational music of mainstream culture during the reign of the big bands in the forties.)

"Carolina shouts" actually were often plaintive cries for relief in this world or for redemption in the next, as shown by this South Carolina chain-gang song:

> Lawd, I'm goin' down to Columbia
> Goin' to fall down, fall down on my knees
> I'm goin' to ax the hard-hearted governor
> Will he pardon me, pardon me, if he please
> "No pardon for you, partner, you got to make your time . . ."
> Don't talk about it, 'bout it, if you do I'll cry,
> Don't talk about it, 'bout it, if you do I'll die.

The carefree ditties and dances of the "roaring twenties" were expressions of youthful exuberance distilled, in part, from the heaviest despair.

Romantic nostalgia for plantations, pickaninnies, and other symbols of the Old South shaped the design of culture in the twenties. The profound paradoxes and troubling memories at the heart of the southern experience, while not resolved in the minds of either most black or white people, were irreverently and cathartically expressed as "Dixie to Broadway" motifs in popular American music, advertising, graphic arts, dance, theater, and idiomatic speech. While the popu-larity of jazz styles helped to counteract the grotesqueries of minstrelsy, stereotyp-ical imagery of black people persisted, and while the styles and products of black improvisation were widely emulated, the creators were often ignored or shunned.

A culmination of trends generated by African American improvisation and American technological innovation in the twenties occurred with the production in 1927 of the first full-length "talking picture": *The Jazz Singer* starring Al Jolson, the last titan of blackface.

"Fascinatin' rhythm" enthralls the nation: black style sans black people: the latest sensation!

Blackface became black voice as radio and Amos and Andy supplanted vaude-ville and burnt-cork minstrelsy as a staple of American entertainment in the thirties.

A major force in the creation of popular culture during the tens, twenties, and thirties flowed through the Jewish-African American connection. Elements of rhythmic, resonant sympathy, as well as appropriation, exploitation, and cap-italization, as well as mutually (but not necessarily *equally* mutual) advantageous syntheses and symbioses between "black creativity," "white power," and Jewish *chutzpah* combined in the production of this era's mass entertainment. Jolson's caricatures were, it seems to me, distortions of a Near Eastern Semitic affinity for sister Africa. Irving Berlin, George M. Cohen, Sigmund Romberg, George and Ira Gershwin, Oscar Hammerstein, and other Jewish, jazz-influenced creators of American popular music perhaps still felt some resonance of the beat from East Africa and Egypt through the ancient intercultural Near East—a resonance suf-fused with the soulful expression of their own suffering people.

The soul in the machine, 1930s: Jazz navigators drove a tighter, more propulsive and streamlined engine during the "swing era," which officially began in 1935 with Benny Goodman's triumphant reception at the Paramount Theater in Los Angeles, following a disappointing national tour. Already swinging to the beat, the L.A. kids had enjoyed optimal access to it during coast-to-coast broad-casts of the Goodman band, which, originating in New York at midnight, aired during prime time in the West.

The concept and style of swing had been definitively expressed some years before by Louis Armstrong, Fletcher Henderson, and others. Duke Ellington wrote and arranged "It Don't Mean a Thing" in 1931, recording it in February 1932. Advancing a primary principle of the philosophy of swing as originally set forth in a verbally rapped credo by musician Bubber Miley—"It don't mean a thing, if it ain't got that swing"—the credo-inspired piece, wrote Ellington, became "famous as the expression of a sentiment which prevailed among jazz musicians at that time."[10]

Jazz propulsion peaked on the "A Train." The automated yet syncopated style of the Ellington-Strayhorn composition expressed rhythms not only of Harlem, not only of modern Manhattan, but also of the soul of the machinery—the transcultural core of North American industrial manpower and might.

An evolving, self-validating African American feminine persona found dis-tinctive musical expression in the styles of swing. In 1918, at demonstrations at a Chicago music store, teasin' brown Lil Hardin's imaginative flair on the piano shone as bright as any promenade of mulatto pulchritude on the Orpheum circuit.

In the first decades of the twentieth century, self-invention was necessary for free-spirited, young African American women. There were no models for how to be authentic—not the white women whom they worked for, not the tentative personas of their mothers' generation, not the abused and triumphantly don't-bit-mo'-care personas of Mamie, Bessie, Clara and the other early bluesmiths.

After Benny Goodman was crowned "king of swing," Ella Fitzgerald ascended the queen's throne singing "A Tisket, A Tasket." Fitzgerald's sweet and sassy way with the tune and its theme were culminations of the frisky rhythms and styles of little black girls' games such as "Lil Sally Walker": *Shake it to the east. Shake it to the west. Shake it to the one that you love the best.* The games were syntheses of inherited conventions: antebellum "setting the flo'" dance moves ("goin' to the east / goin' to the west"); the "Ballin' the Jack" song and dance of the 1900s ("shake your hips, let your backbone slip"); and typical little-black-girl playground sass. Fitzgerald's insouciant plea for her "little yellow basket" projected the sound of a new, prototypical African American femininity beyond sweet swinging to sweet and supreme jive.

> Billie Holiday was Ella's accomplice in crime.
> Only Lady was more stubborn and daring
> as she caressed the off-beats and made them sublime.

Billie, Ella, Louis, Duke, King Oliver, Buddy Bolden—signifiers all. "Signifyin'" can be either a subtle or bodacious way of showing off. What young black musicians had been showing off, ever since before ragtime, was something that black folk abundantly possessed, something that was just as clever and scintillating as any white man's marvel. Signifyin', through the masterful strokes of swing, helped to produce a healthy equilibrium in the land—a spunky, high-spirited contradiction by black musicians of the distorted, demeaning conceptions of black people in mass media and popular opinion. But, first of all and after all, jazz innovators swung as a way of flying, to their own astonished satisfaction and delight.

> Signification was a repudiation of spoofs on spooks
> on everything from matchbooks to billboards:
> ogling dandies and grinning black baboons
> purporting—lying through their teeth—to be *us*.
> We were not amused. Our highest aspiration was to be "for real."

Swing's laid back yet intense forward drive embraced all: The Ellington band's jungle rhythms of the early thirties, Goodman's tight, bouncing, grandly orchestrated riffs of the mid to late thirties, and Basie's blast from the West. (From jumpin' at the woodpile to the Woodside [Hotel]—a fabulous leap, leaving everybody in the dust.) Swing rolled on to impel the thundering boogie-woogie of Pete Johnson, Albert Ammons, and Meade Lux Lewis and to color the artistries of Stan Kenton before passing over in to an immortalized form of instrumental American popular music, forever after.

Through the worse days of lynching and Jim Crow segregation, through the worse dying days of minstrelsy, black folk *took* their propers, thank you, and gave them back through amazing gifts of improvisation and feeling: rhythm and blues—gifts paid by plenty dues.

Conceiving of the human environment as rhythmic in its configurations and patterns and in its breaks and intervals, it is not hard to imagine the physical structures of contemporary urban poverty (concrete landscape, windows onto walls, high-rise sardine stacks, overcrowding, dilapidation) as a kind of enervating stases—forms mostly devoid of life-giving properties through and over which the hard-core school of rap struggles to prevail. In lyric and tone, just as deadening, repetitious, and mechanical as the artificial and often stultifying environment from which it emerges, the hard core reclaims almighty raw rhythm as its formidable weapon of resistance.

As suggested by its name, rap collectively constitutes a conversation—a literal discourse—between its various schools: basic hip hop, Jamaican (a mix of African, East Indian, and Cockney *flavas*), sun-fried Atlanta/southern, northeastern boho, Long Beach/New Jack, Gospel, Latin, etc. Collectively rapped discourse is built upon a simple, repetitious beat. Similarly, "artistic" schools strive to elevate jazz- and blues-inspired improvisational values in their execution of rhythmic variations and the "nihilistic" schools ride the repetitious, monotonous beat unwaveringly *hard* as an expression of pure, personal force—a singular, macho assertion of self over all else. Distinctive elements of rap's various schools are converging—the result of innovative, imaginative appropriations—in some of the latest samples.

Hard-core rap's concentration on elemental rhythms and droning drivel echoes the enchanting monotonous chants of the old praise houses and the primal, jive bravura of early R&B dj's. The power of all syncopated rhythm, from elemental to advanced, lies in its ability to rock one's entire being: it feels good to the body and irresistibly evokes response; it excites the mind and, being a language that directly speaks to spirit, comforts the soul. Ironically, the hard core of the music now called "rock" rages in grinding tonal intensity and volume but not in interestingly patterned rhythm. The effect is deadening to people who appreciate originality in rhythmic expression.

The most outrageously inventive "rhythming" (Duke's word) is today being created by gospel composers, arrangers, singers, and musicians. An exciting element of contemporary gospel music is its emphatic asymmetry in tone and beat. Sanctified rhythm, indeed.

Now, as always, rhythm is a primary improvisational tool for black people, most particularly for those who lack access to other empowering resources. When no ways out of a bad situation can be directly found, they are improvised. *All God's chillun' got rhythm!*

CHAPTER TWO

JAZZ TIME AND
OUR TIME | *A View from the Outside In*

MARK SUMNER HARVEY

In one view of creativity, art is an attempt to impose order on nature and culture. Order in music is imposed through form and structure, performance practice, and audience expectation. Certainly one of the chief aspects of this process is the use of rhythm. Rhythm measures the flow of musical time and orders it through metrical demarcation. In addition, pattern and accent further define the sense of order for composer, performer, and listener alike.

In jazz, time is all important. By this jazz people usually mean a steady propulsive flow of beats as with swing rhythm, most typically anchored by a solid walking bass line and crisp yet relaxed cymbal work. The trick is to maintain a comfortable groove while injecting tension and contrast into the rhythmic stream. This is true whatever the rhythmic "feel" engaged (swing, funk, Latin, etc.) or whatever the tempo. But there is more to it than this. As Anthony Braxton has said, "Tempo is a limited use of time. I think of time as *all* the time."[1]

What if time in music, specifically jazz, is thought of and heard as *all* the time? What would this mean and what would this sound like? Certainly considerations of tempo, groove, flow, "feel," tension, contrast, pattern and accent and even meter would not be cast aside but rather reconfigured. Some larger notion of rhythm's function as part of musical art might also emerge. Perhaps the urge for order is not art's only *raison d'être,* perhaps not even its most significant one. Or perhaps there are several conceptions of order and variant ways in which music (and other art forms) may express them, lending possible insights to aspects of individual and social life.

I write these musings from the outside in, that is, as a jazz performer, composer and historian committed to an expansive, exploratory and inclusive perspective on this music. This means I value the entire sweep of the jazz tradition, including the free jazz or "outside" movement which has been largely ignored, obscured or excommunicated from "the tradition" since the eighties. And it will be this movement and its subsequent generation of practitioners on which I will focus in this essay. For far from being an aberration, this movement has been and continues to be a rich vein of creative musical activity.[2]

This is particularly so when considered in terms of rhythm and time. These aspects of music cannot really be separated out from others; however, they will provide the focus for my observations within a larger musical context. I will consider the questions concerning order and time posed above through an interpretation of three musical illustrations. Two of John Coltrane's recorded versions of "My Favorite Things" will be compared in order to explore the structure and play of time. Also, the recording *America-South Africa* by the Art Ensemble of Chicago will be examined for the ways it exemplifies this group's orientation toward creating ritual time. Along the way I hope to shed some light on the participation of both players and listeners in the improvisational experience.

John Coltrane was and remains a seminal figure in modern jazz. While not an iconoclast like Ornette Coleman, Coltrane evolved into an avant-gardist. He sought both musical and spiritual truth, and his pilgrimage is chronicled in his many recordings, especially those he made during the last decade of his life following his religious awakening in 1957.[3]

Coltrane's first recording of Rodgers and Hammerstein's "My Favorite Things," from *The Sound of Music,* was also the first recording he made with the players who had created the chemistry his music needed to really soar: McCoy Tyner on piano, Elvin Jones on drums, and Steve Davis in the bass chair, to be succeeded by Reggie Workman, then Jimmy Garrison. While the album *My Favorite Things*[4] announced this quartet and the leader's performance on soprano saxophone (an instrument previously overlooked by reed players) and was enormously popular, its title tune is a highly distinctive and special exploration of the complexity of time.

The 1960 version of "My Favorite Things" seems fairly straightforward upon first hearing, although, as Eric Nisenson has observed, "images of Julie Andrews and those lovable nuns and kids vanished moments into [it]."[5] The basic theme is stated at the beginning and end of the piece with solos in the middle—a conventional theme-and-variations approach. But closer listening reveals far greater complexity. Coltrane fragments the full tune, giving only the first sixteen-measure section several times over as the opening "head" while closing by playing that same section once, and then, for the first and only time, presenting the third section of the song (for those who may know the lyrics, at the line "When the dog bites, when the bee stings . . ."). Furthermore, the tune is rendered modally rather than harmonically; that is, a two-chord vamp and two modes or scales—one minor, the other major—provide the materials by which the piece is recomposed.

In terms of the structure of time these are radical reconfigurations. Coltrane knew of Ornette Coleman's similar yet even more daring experiments, had recorded an album with Coleman's sidemen a few months earlier, and had been exploring modal approaches with the Miles Davis band of the later fifties. So the structuring process was not entirely new but neither was it occurring in a vacuum.

The modal approach itself was radical. Although some of the chord changes are implied whenever the melody is played, harmonic structure is largely dissolved, and with it harmonic rhythm. This is the rhythm that dictates how chords progress, how melodic phrases are contextualized, and how the larger sections of the tune are divided up into smaller subsections, usually providing balance and complementarity. This element of musical structure is eminently logical and clearly similar to harmonic rhythmic practice in Western music.

What Coltrane did by recasting "My Favorite Things" in modal fashion was to subvert this logical structure. He kept just enough of the pattern—sixteen-bar sections of the principal melody, for instance—to maintain connectedness with the original and to provide familiarity to the listeners. However, the solo sections are anchored only by the vamp and one of the two modes. Therefore, the duration of each solo is no longer dictated by the harmonic rhythm or the given form of the piece. Time as duration now must be "created." A new "logic" must be devised to carry forward the "development" of the musical statement.

But why bother about logic and development, at least in conventional terms? This musical movement to modality was about something quite different. For Coltrane and others, it opened up new conceptions of musical meaning. Time as that which is "created" rather than measured or controlled is an essentially African concept.[6] It allows musicians and listeners the opportunity to meditate or ruminate rather than intellectually and aurally follow the cyclical chord progression. It takes both musicians and listeners on an excursion into relatively uncharted waters rather than on a course plotted by charts and channel markers. And it appeals perhaps more to the adventurous than to those more comfortable with familiar territory. And yet, with the foundation of vamp and modes as well as the recurrent statement of the main melody, there is accessibility within the exploratory process. In fact, these melodic markers serve almost as a thematic image in a dream might, to provide a touchstone of reality within surreality.

The original song is set forth in three sections: A, which is the main melody of sixteen measures, repeated a second time after a two measure vamp; B, which is the same melody, also sixteen measures (not repeated) but harmonized in a major tonality to contrast with the overall minor tonality of A; and C, which is a contrasting melody of twenty-four measures (the final four being in the nature of a vamp once again) and with chords that change every two measures rather than every measure, as with A and B. This is an unusual song structure yet one whose basic elements follow accepted models.

The Coltrane version opens with a brief vamp and then presents A twice with an eight-measure vamp in between. This is followed not by B, but by a twenty-four measure solo in the major mode. Next the head is played again, twice in succession, followed by a second brief solo for sixteen measures in the minor mode. This seems very much compatible with the structure of the blues, wherein a phrase is repeated twice then answered. It is especially resonant with the earliest folk or country blues, which often stayed in the same tonality throughout or changed in ways far different than later twelve-bar harmonic forms would allow, often asymmetrically, as is the case here with the opening statement. Whether Coltrane heard or conceived the tune in this way I do not know. But it almost seems that consciously or unconsciously a blues "head" framework has been superimposed on both the original song form and the rhythmic vamp arrangement devised by Coltrane. Further, this rhythmic vamp is significant in its own right, for it overlays a cross-rhythmic feeling on the basic jazz waltz pattern, although, with the redoubtable polyrhythmic wizardry of Elvin Jones in the mix, much more than this is always going on.

Following this opening portion, there come two extended solo sections. McCoy Tyner has the first, Coltrane the second. Tyner's piano solo is remarkable for its rhythmic orientation. He uses the vamp figure as his point of departure, sometimes revoicing chords and clusters derived from the minor mode, occasionally worrying a single-note pattern into minimalist-like repetition or stating the main melody in paraphrase. This solo is not developmental in the traditional sense of a variation on the theme (or form) that spins out new ideas based on melody or harmony. It serves rather to entrance the listener through the repetition of the vamp figure and to drive home the awareness that this is no ordinary interpretation of a Broadway show tune. It also sets the stage for Coltrane's solo section.

When Coltrane enters for his solo, he restates the main melody, then launches forth on a lengthy exploration on the melodic/rhythmic possibilities inherent in the tune. As J. C. Thomas has noted, the playing is full of "frequent trills and arabesques."[7] But it is no more the standard variation-on-a-theme approach than was Tyner's. Thomas has given some important insights into this new method:

> Coltrane is not an artist you can listen to casually. You must give him your undivided attention to even begin to appreciate his talent. He emits a stream of musical consciousness that could, I suppose, be likened to some of the writings of James Joyce. He produces music that might be incomprehensible to some listeners, but its value and meaning lie in his compulsion to weave an entire piece of musical cloth almost instantaneously.[8]

That is, there is a different time sense at work here. Stream of consciousness, time created in the musical process, spontaneity determining duration—these are not easy concepts to grasp, yet they are easily heard in this piece.

In fact, Coltrane gives not one but two solos in this manner. No sooner does he conclude the first and restate the main melody than he is off again on an even more energetic flight of sonic fancy. This time the major mode is favored as his playing waxes ever more active, intricate and dynamically brilliant. The highest range of the soprano sax is pushed, and we hear intimations of his searching "cry," the sound that moves to the boundary of acceptable sound, breaking as it reaches for the ineffable expression of what his soul is experiencing. Coltrane's phrases in this second solo are the most free of allegiance to patterns implied by the original tune and even his recasting of it in this arrangement. His own cross-rhythmic playing extends and intensifies the tension prefigured by the rhythmic vamp. Yet it is all very human music, perhaps because the saxophonist must breathe. And so, even at its most turbulent, it says something we who also must breathe can understand.

To conclude, the piece returns to a final statement of the main melody answered by the final section C of the original tune, and some last comments and trills by Coltrane that fade into an Elvin Jones decrescendo return us to ourselves, perhaps illuminated or transformed, however fleetingly.

Structurally, the analogy to the blues "head" no longer holds with this ending. But this is not, after all, a piece concerned with conventional approaches, and so an outright recapitulation of an imputed blues format need not occur. However, the manner in which the principal structural sections are arranged may imply yet another superimposed framework, that of a prism-like refraction of the tune rather than a linear, developmental pattern. To mix metaphors with impunity, it is almost as if the original tune were placed under a microscopic lens so that its inner qualities and potentialities might be seen more clearly. Removing the eye from the microscope and focusing again on phenomenal reality, a sense of having waked from a dream may well be present. That is, a different time has been experienced visually in this metaphor and aurally in Coltrane's recomposition of the tune. Aspects of African polyrhythm, blues form, imaginative improvisation, and much more blend in a nearly fourteen-minute musical piece that often seems either far shorter or far longer to this listener each time he hears it.

By the time Coltrane recorded "My Favorite Things" for the last time in May 1966, a little over a year before he died, his aesthetic conception and his band had changed dramatically.[9] Yet there was continuity with what had come before. As his explorations of the avant-garde, or New Thing, intensified in the sixties, there finally came a point where both Elvin Jones and McCoy Tyner had to part company with Coltrane. Bassist Jimmy Garrison, on board for some years, remained in his pivotal role, joined by Rashied Ali on drums, John's wife Alice Coltrane on piano, a young Pharoah Sanders on tenor sax, and, for the Village Vanguard club date at which this version of "My Favorite Things" was recorded, an additional percussionist, Emanuel Rahim.

Although the music this group created was far more tumultuous and controversial than what had come before, it was really only extending the approaches and overall conception set in motion by performances such as the one described above. The 1966 version of "My Favorite Things" is similar to the 1960 version in that the basic A melody is referred to often and the C section is heard once again only at the conclusion of the entire piece. But there are many differences.

Jimmy Garrison begins with an unaccompanied bass solo, slightly over five minutes long, which acts as a prelude, perhaps "quieting the mind" for what will follow. Then Coltrane on soprano sax begins his improvisatory flight over a solid bass vamp which is quickly thickened by an overlay of percussive piano and drum work that is not polyrhythmic so much as poly-pulsational. Nearly three minutes of this soloistic/textural fabric evolve before the main melody (A) is heard for the first time, and it springs forth cleanly and clearly from the density preceding it as if by sorcery. In fact, the musicians felt the basic pulse underlying all of the complex rhythmic activity, even though it was not stated as such. A quick nod from the leader most likely gave the exact cue into the melody. Still, it is a wonderful and most amazing moment.

This format is repeated three more times, increasingly energetic improvisation punctuated by bursts of melody, each repetition finding Coltrane shortening his solo asymmetrically, yet such that a kind of logical proportioning seems to be at work. This whole section of saxophone and ensemble lasts well over six minutes and certainly cannot be compared even remotely with the more conventional theme-and-variations approach. In this performance we have something more closely resembling pure improvisation, with bits of melody interjected at ever smaller intervals. And this is not quite the halfway point.

Coltrane then pushes even farther. The music is still being created in time, but it is really being created, without much predetermined material, in "all the time," to recall Anthony Braxton's piquant phrase. Tempo and meter, pattern and accent, syncopation and polyrhythm are all vastly less important to this new conception. They are dissolved, along with harmonic rhythm, in a sea of rhythmic/melodic/textural possibility. J. C. Thomas has written one of the best descriptions of this conception; he is speaking of Coltrane's saxophone style, but his words apply to the broader aesthetic as well:

> His melodic lines are like a wave effect, each new musical explosion cresting, then collapsing, then cresting again, this time more powerful than the preceding wave. And that is only the surface of his sound, as the waves are only external manifestations of the ocean. . . . For he is a time traveler; his music is of the past and future tenses as well as the present. He takes the listener back to a time when the earth's crust was barely cooled and the sea creatures had not yet begun their long walk on the land; and forward to an era yet uncharted and unpredicted where music may be transmitted from mind to mind in such an instantaneous accomplishment that there will no longer be any need for musical instruments as such.[10]

The rhythm of waves cresting and collapsing is a most apt metaphor by which to describe and hear this music. Time is played, and is to be listened to as if it were something surrounding us, something of which we are a part, something filling us with awe. Control and measurement hardly seem of consequence any longer.

Thomas characterizes Coltrane as a "time traveler," and perhaps this is so. Eric Nisenson notes, "As his music became freer, Coltrane increasingly took on the role of shaman, not just playing his horn but now leading a quasi-religious ritual."[11] Part of this ritual was his own incessant need to be connected with the sound by playing small percussion instruments when not soloing, moving animatedly or even whirling around the stage, occasionally pounding his chest "while vocally roaring at the top of his lungs."[12] Perhaps this was an attempt to effect what Mircea Eliade has termed a "technique of ecstasy," resulting among authentic shamans in the ability to see spirits, to become a spirit and leave one's body, to travel through time and space.[13] It is certainly the case that many observers detected something of this quest, if not its realization. Edward Strickland described Coltrane's music as a "search for the rhythmic equivalent of the oceanic feeling of visionary experience" and felt that the explanation for his move into the avant-garde was that he "forsook lyricism for an unfettered quest for ecstasy."[14] C. O. Simpkins said this about the audiences' responses to the music of this later period:

> The usual pattern was that first those who didn't appreciate the music left. For those who stayed, the music was affecting them in some way. There were those who jumped straight up in the air, shouting 'arrghhhh!' with their hands over their ears and running out of the club. The music would be bringing out all the bad parts of themselves and confronting them with it. They would come back inside to receive more exorcism. . . . Some just held their heads over to the side, letting the music carry them to paradise. Still others frantically danced and tapped along with the music on improvised instruments of tables and glasses. It was a religious experience for many, and the lines to the door of the clubs were always long.[15]

This was indeed a religious experience, and one very much in keeping with the shamanistic curative function. But it was a costly business, entailing sacrifice for the musician-*cum*-shaman who suffered with cancer (part of his "initiatory sickness" perhaps?) and died just a few months shy of his forty-first birthday. And doubtless frustrating, as Nisenson surmises while discussing how club owners and patrons opposed to this more radical music often demanded familiar "tunes":

> Since his career was tied directly to a quest that was personal and metaphysical as well as musical, such demands must have been severely disappointing to Coltrane. They showed that a large segment of his audience was ignorant of the enormous amount of sacrifice and continual inner growth, as well as the purely physical wear, that went into developing an art that he believed would yield great spiritual revelation and ultimate insight into the nature of man and his universe, rather than just a moment's entertainment.[16]

Yet how could it be otherwise? Coltrane and all the other experimentalists of this period were recasting not only the music but also the time-space context within which it took place. That is why much of this music moved from the clubs to lofts, art galleries, churches, and community centers. A performance such as the one being discussed here was investing the Vanguard with a sacral aura for the duration of the event. This clashed tremendously with the commercial, entertainment expectations of listeners who wanted "a good time" rather than an opportunity to participate in a propitious summoning of spirits.

But let us return to the piece itself. After the bass solo and extended solo/ensemble portion mentioned above, a brief piano interlude is heard. Then comes more than eleven minutes of marvelously frenzied playing by both Pharoah Sanders and Coltrane. Roughly the second half of this twenty-one-minute opus is improvisational sonic exploration definitely not for the faint of heart. Sanders begins with a tenor sax solo slightly more than three minutes long, which merges into a duet with Coltrane, now playing bass clarinet. This solo and duet pattern recurs, out of which emerges Coltrane, now playing soprano sax, for a four-minute solo, his longest in the piece. As the solo fades and cools down the intense heat generated in the preceding section, the C section of the tune appears, bringing the powerful and overwhelming musical event to its conclusion.

Many listeners, then and now, heard or hear only turmoil, ugliness, a sense of the grotesque, and even chaos in this music—and not just in this piece, but with others that carry more self-conscious imagery of spiritual quest, such as *Ascension* and *The Father and the Son and the Holy Ghost.* Indeed, after his 1964 masterpiece, *A Love Supreme,* until his demise in 1967, little of Coltrane's music easily fits the conventional characterization of "spiritual." Yet the artist intended it to be regarded as such and it was clearly perceived as such by those quoted above and by dedicated Coltrane fans.

The music of this last period of Coltrane's life was spiritual in nature not because Coltrane had attained absolute serenity but because his continuous struggle and search for it was so honest and focused. As Kierkegaard said, "Purity of heart is to will one thing." In his personal quest, Coltrane followed that willed purpose through many dimensions of aesthetic and human experience. Nat Hentoff, commenting on "The Father and the Son and the Holy Ghost," observed:

> It is as if [Coltrane] and Sanders were speaking with "the gift of tongues"—as if their insights were of such compelling force that they have to transcend ordinary ways of musical speech and ordinary textures to be able to convey that part of the essence of being they have touched. The emotions . . . must explode as felt—in the rawness of palpable, visceral, painful, challenging, scraping, scouring self-discovery. For there to be unity, there must first be a plunge into and through the agony of separateness.[17]

And all of this applies equally well to "My Favorite Things" from this same period. For Coltrane's music was cut from the same cloth, regardless of the particular title image given to a specific piece. Undoubtedly each composition or interpretation had special personal meaning for him, but each in its own way served as a vehicle for his relentless searching after truth and beauty, even if his musical expression redefined these very terms.

That is part of the reason the pieces were so long. They were enactments of the process of self-discovery, not merely the refined product distilled into a representation of the activity. Coltrane's recorded performances, although marketable as music industry product, are really this activity itself. They may still be heard not only as processes of his own self-discovery, but as evolutionary streams that invite us as listeners inside and into the depths of our own life experience. That is why these late works are not readily understood or appreciated; their power is literally overwhelming, too much to bear or to hear.

But these are musical works meaningful not only on a personal level. They are also significant on a wider plane, that of culture and consciousness. The movement away from measured "jazz time" to a rhythmical sense that was multidirectional and a conceptual sense of time as oceanic, vast and creative, portended much. Such shifts were part of larger changes of that time period, oriented toward new configurations and meanings for art, politics, religion, and other aspects of spiritual and cultural life.

Here the words of Erich Neumann on the subject of art and time are especially instructive:

> In our age, as never before, truth implies the courage to face chaos. . . . But it is a total misunderstanding of our time and our art to regard their relation to chaos as purely negative. . . . Conscious renunciation of form is often falsely interpreted as inability to give form, as incompetence. Actually, the breakdown of consciousness, carrying the artist backward to an all-embracing *participation* with the world, contains the constructive, creative elements of a new world vision.[18]

With these admonitions that recall Levy-Bruhl's notion of the *participation mystique* and Jung's belief in the transpersonal nature of artistic creation,[19] Neumann further elucidates the importance of time for art.

The image of the artist being carried backward is again that of the time traveler, the shaman. Renunciation of form is due neither to inability nor to incompetence but may well portend a shift in the center of gravity from consciousness of what is "toward a creative matrix where something new is in preparation."[20] But to fully appreciate this change, we must be willing also to confront its negative aspect, willing to have "the courage to face chaos." We must not do so just to move past this stage on to resolution and the new. We must also do this in order to fully understand what is happening within this chaos and to glean what lessons we may from it. As Neumann says, "The disintegration and dissonance of this art are our own; to understand them is to understand ourselves."[21] And to regard them as significant elements of the whole process toward creative breakthrough, rather than as something to be summarily put off or away, is part of wisdom.

Some of those described by Simpkins who heard Coltrane in a club setting felt that this disintegration and dissonance provoked a kind of exorcism, while others let the music "carry them to paradise." Coltrane himself wanted to produce beautiful, uplifting music—music that would do things to people "that they need," music that would "make them happy."[22] Although listeners had described his music as "angry," "tortured," or "overpowering," he summarized his own view as follows:

> You never know where it's going to go. All a musician can do is
> get closer to the sources of nature, and so feel that he is in communion
> with the natural laws. Then he can feel that he is interpreting them to
> the best of his ability, and can try to convey that to others.[23]

This suggests a range of responses to and resonances with Coltrane's music. It also suggests that both artist and audience may be susceptible to multiple, even simultaneous, emotional and expressive states. That is, in this music we can hear both the chaos and its confrontation, both the renunciation of old forms and the birth of new ones. I believe this explains why Coltrane could hold this tension and literally embody its creative dynamic in his music. It also may explain why many listeners could hear the beauty where others could only recognize the pain in the very act of transformation.

On the larger transpersonal level, this was also the case, as Coltrane and a significant minority of other imaginative musicians experimented with new approaches in search of what Neumann called "the constructive, creative elements of a new world vision." And by renouncing time-bound forms and rhythms, they were able to develop an art that spoke most directly to its time.

Coltrane and the other adventurers of the sixties were part of a *zeitgeist* that included the assassinations of John and Robert Kennedy, Martin Luther King, Jr., and Malcolm X, the bombings of black churches and schoolhouses, the murders of black and white civil-rights workers, the growing involvement of America in the Vietnam War, and the growth of a youth counterculture and a resurgent feminist movement among so many other patterns and pieces of a society in flux—or in chaos, depending on one's political or cultural viewpoint. The music of this avant-garde movement within jazz reclaimed the position of the early modern avant-garde arts, as a force and a presence sharing in the transformation of that time.

But what of our time, and jazz time? Significant ripple effects in both consciousness and culture continue to emanate from that earlier period of the sixties, and Coltrane continues to be venerated, although much less so for his daring exploratory phase. However, trends and changes in musical fashion unimaginable thirty years ago have led to a situation oriented toward nostalgia and comfort. Largely uncomfortable with our present, many look to the past for meaning or for models upon which to base contemporary events. Thus we have at our disposal, in many idioms, retro-movements based variously in the fifties, sixties, or seventies.

A similar situation obtains in the jazz field: repertory jazz orchestras, with sartorial and aesthetic tastes reflective of the fifties and some aspects of the sixties and an interest in older forms, either in and of themselves or as models for contemporary expression. This implies a renewed interest in harmonic rhythm, form-dictated improvisation, and a basic theme-and-variations approach. Performance durations are much shorter, rarely more than the six- or seven-minute musical "bite" necessary for radio airplay of the "product." And most of the popular jazz artists of today, young and old alike, tend to work from a solid rhythmic underpinning—in time and tempo, the all-important feeling of groove. Finally, most of this music is presented for "a good time," even when complementary educational and canon-creating concerns are also manifest, as in the programs of colleges and major arts institutions.

All of this is highly significant. It signals that jazz has truly become enshrined as an art form. It indicates a maturation of sorts, after about a century of rapid evolution, which allows for musicians and listeners to range across most of the jazz spectrum, much as classical players and aficionados do. And it proves as never before how truly American this music is, celebrating tunes that are relatively accessible, rhythms that are steady, and often texts that speak to us in a variety of ways. The well-deserved "rediscovery" of Tony Bennett by the MTV generation is but one salient proof of this doctrine.

But these same trends are significant because the urgency and energy of the more adventurous music of thirty-odd years ago seems to have diminished greatly if not disappeared altogether in some quarters. Coltrane's 1960 version of "My Favorite Things" continues to be widely admired and emulated while the 1966 version speaks to a much smaller audience. It is as if what might be termed a kind of basic research has not been acknowledged in the developing theory and practice of this art form. This runs counter to the more general pattern of jazz history, one of experimentation then incorporation of new ideas.

As noted earlier, both nostalgia and comfort are popular longings that help explain this situation. The social and political conservatism of recent years is also a factor as an urge for order and control has become more palpable. And there is certainly some correlation between that and the reaffirmation of order, control, form, and general manageability, if not predictability, in contemporary jazz styles and tastes.

Yet in the face, or perhaps the ear, of all this security-conscious music making in jazz (and in the classical sphere as well), there have been some who choose to continue along the trajectories charted in the sixties. A few of the original explorers are still at it, notably Cecil Taylor and Ornette Coleman. And although the near-mythic presences of Coltrane and Sun Ra have passed from our midst, others carry on the work. Among these are Anthony Braxton, Butch Morris, Marilyn Crispell, and Muhal Richard Abrams, founder in 1965 of the Association for the Advancement of Creative Musicians, one of the pivot-points of the "second generation" avant-garde movement based in Chicago. And arguably the most decisively important group to emerge from the AACM was the Art Ensemble of Chicago.

The Art Ensemble, like the AACM, consciously omitted the term *jazz* as a modifier, not as a statement of renunciation, but simply to denote a wider ambit with many options available. Over the course of their almost thirty years together, the members of the AEC have indeed cooked up one of the most eclectic musical gumbos imaginable. They have also blended better than any other group the principal threads and themes of the earlier avant-garde movement, namely concerns for aesthetic and technical experimentation and political and cultural relevance, all spiritually grounded.

What they do has to be seen and heard to be believed. Here is a description by Larry Birnbaum that will serve to begin to relate the AEC to the subject of this essay:

> The currents of African and Eastern spiritualism figure heavily in the group's world outlook. . . . The Eastern conception of the mystical unity of all being is reflected in the organic unity with which the group integrates its disparate influences, in the ebb and flow of their seamless programs. . . . The total effect is hypnotic, ethereal—one is lifted out of mundane reality onto a higher plane.[24]

Particularly with the mention of a conception that is both organic and hypnotic, the aesthetic of Coltrane's later music is evoked, for his influence is one of many foundational guideposts for this ensemble. But this group has transmuted that basic orientation to include not just free jazz but the spectrum of jazz styles and black music—Gospel, blues, r&b, folk forms—as well as many world music and classical influences. The second half of their tag line "Great Black Music: Ancient to the Future" provides the self-conscious warrant for their time travel. In the passage quoted above, we are told that in their programs "one is lifted out of mundane reality onto a higher plane." In other words, the AEC is continuing the shamanistic approach noted earlier and doing so through a most skillful appreciation of, respect for, and use of time. Most engagingly, the group members understand the deep meaning of both the play of time and how to play within time, often injecting humor into music making of high purpose and achievement.

Stuart Broomer, writing in a review of CD reissues of early recordings (from 1967 and 1968), provides further insight into their work:

> Improvised music is itself a ceremony of freedom, but the music of the Art Ensemble was becoming more openly ceremonial. . . . This sense of ceremony . . . tends to treat musical space and time as ritual space and sacred time.[25]

Broomer simply tosses off that wonderful phrase, "Improvised music is itself a ceremony of freedom," but I will have more to say about that below. Now I want to address this notion of "ritual space and sacred time" to which he alludes.

The ceremonial aspect of the Art Ensemble's performances is inescapable. For many years the group has appeared in costume, favoring dashikis and face paint and headdresses, with trumpeter Lester Bowie attired in his white laboratory technician's coat. The enormous panoply of instruments they use can fill most orchestral stages, presenting an intoxicating forest of sound possibilities to the eye, then to the ear as various of them are called into play. Not all presentations merit full regalia or instrumentation, yet any and all concerts are likely to be both entertaining and edifying on many levels.

Even more important than these factors is the use of space and time. The physical presence of the musicians is situated in a space but so also are their sounds. Indeed, space is often synonymous with silence, the space between or in and around the sounds. Speaking of a precursor group to the AEC, in which Roscoe Mitchell and other soon-to-be Art Ensemble members played, John Litweiler has said:

> What the Mitchell Sextet did in "Sound" was to return music to its very basis: the discovery and relation of sounds within the natural force of silence.[26]

And it was perhaps more than anything else the respect for silence or space that set the AEC apart from many of the sixties and seventies avant-gardists. As with the Chinese and Japanese concept of *Ma*—the void or empty space, silence can be very full when properly understood and "heard." Further, when sounds are placed within this space or silence, they take on new significance. Much Art Ensemble music explores this dynamic, often producing pieces better thought of as "sound structures" that use tone color and texture rather than melody, harmony, and rhythm in any conventional sense.[27]

Balancing and complementing this approach, the AEC also employs clearly melodic and rhythmic elements, often settling into quite infectious grooves. But it is the way these elements are set within larger structural wholes that lends them a kind of dramatic effect and power all their own. A cursory listening to a recent CD, *America–South Africa*, will provide but one of many possible illustrations of this perspective.[28]

The title of this CD is very direct, and the opening selection has lyrics that drive home the point even more forcefully: "two different lands / yet somehow the same." The AEC changed its name for this recording to take into account its political character and to be more inclusive of the accompanying musicians, the Amabutho Male Chorus of South Africa. Thus, this particular CD goes under the banner of "The Art Ensemble of Soweto," and the cover art is a photo of the five AEC players in their full ceremonial dress.

While the recording is divided into six sections, individually titled, it is really one long musical statement. The first and fourth pieces are the longest, about eighteen and fourteen minutes respectively, with the other four about three, four, or five minutes long. But the recording takes shape as one extended forty-six-minute work. And, most importantly, within that duration it creates its own unique ritual time and space.

This work, from 1991, before the end of apartheid, is quite obviously about a political subject, suggesting an equal oppression for black people in the United States and the Union of South Africa. It begins with a vocal chant—"U.S. of A.— U. of S.A."—sung by the Art Ensemble and the Amabutho Male Chorus (who also play percussion and keyboards elsewhere). This brief, pointed incantation is followed by some equally brief bursts of sound by saxes and trumpet, then a synthesizer vamp begins. This vamp and the accompanying percussion suggest a groove and feeling similar to those that Abdullah Ibrahim, himself a South African expatriate, has made popular. The vocal group enters again with *America-South Africa,* and then a text by AEC member Joseph Jarman is spoken. Images of poverty, welfare, and killing—"no education for all poor men / all locked up in a cage of pain"—are juxtaposed with a danceable, hypnotic groove.

Next comes a much less defined section with vocal interjections, aleatoric and atmospheric sounds, fragments of melodic ideas, a solo by trumpeter Lester Bowie that never quite takes off in this context, sounds of a siren, and a general air of chaos and turbulence. This is followed by another repeated chant bridging to a rolling tom-tom pattern, with auto "bulb" horns overlaid, as voices name many of the legendary figures in the struggle for liberation: Walter Sisulu, Medgar Evers, Elias Motsaoledi, Martin Luther King, Nelson Mandela, Malcolm X, Rosa Parks, and more. After the narration "these black folks came to show the way," the original groove returns with more exuberant sax and trumpet figures, chants, and then the culminating narration "The time is now, the hour has come; Take up the power, take over the show." The repeated riff-chant "America-South Africa" with swirling accompaniment fades down to close out this first piece.

This is extremely powerful, evocative music or music-event or music-theater documented much as it would be in performance. It is consistent with the Art Ensemble's other work, both musically and philosophically, and uses the text segments as both discursive and melodic-rhythmic textural elements within the composition. Well organized, it also contains many contrasts. Yet it returns at various points in its nearly eighteen-minute duration to chants and rhythmic underpinnings that provide a common thread of continuity and coherence.

But more than this, "U.S. of A.—U. of S.A." engages the listeners in a kind of ritual of its own making. Perhaps this is an impermissible use of the term "ritual," implying as it does tradition and history. Yet if Erich Neumann is right, a time of chaos or disorder will provoke artists, some of them anyway, to creative activity aimed toward addressing that situation and looking forward to some resolution beyond it. The Art Ensemble of Chicago/Soweto, here and elsewhere, has shown itself to be such a collective of artists.

The use of chanted phrases and narration is part of this ritual. It puts us in the mind of time and space travel, ranging across sea and land between America and South Africa and backward into historical memory as a kind of sacred naming ceremony is presented, recalling ancestors and martyrs as well as still-living participants in the struggle for justice and freedom. The musical structure itself is another part of it. The Art Ensemble's declared intention to perform "Great Black Music: Ancient to the Future" is well-displayed here. Rhythm underlies and unites all the disparate elements in this piece. As with traditional African ritual music, there is room in the time and space for individual and smaller-group participation—various fragments and riffs—as well as that which involves the larger group. But, as modernists, the AEC also makes room for a more "abstract" section—which in fact may be very concrete in expressing the turmoil felt inside the narration—and for recurring commentary in this style throughout the larger work. As with the music of John Coltrane, the listener is caught up in the flow of time, taken on a journey or perhaps transported through a rite of passage and then returned to a more prosaic state, ideally unconscious of how much time has elapsed.

However, this is only the beginning. A second and far shorter piece moves into the field of sound and silence discussed above. Marvelous gong, cymbal, and bell sounds take the listener to a new place in the aural imagination as Lester Bowie brings a lovely melody into the foreground. The third piece, also shorter, features a slow-ballad approach at the beginning and end, with a medium-tempo swing in midsection. The horns are more arranged here, and although tempo is employed, it is as often implied as stated. The actual time sense is not strict, and rhythm-section players move in and out of time effortlessly. The fourth composition, much longer at just over fourteen minutes, recalls and continues the mood of the second piece. We hear once again the gong and bell sounds, but this time Bowie explores the "interior" of the trumpet, finding all manner of strange and wonderful sounds. Saxes are added into this mix and then the trumpet soars in lyrical, open fashion. The remainder of the piece, much too long to detail here, is an eloquent elegy in which horn chorale-like lines, *arco* string bass work, various light percussion, and occasional urgent, strident sounds are blended together. This might be heard as the mirror-image of the opening composition, but now we are taken into a reflective, ruminative place, an emotional space often encountered late in the night when questions of risk, cost, and consequence emerge. Such programmatic ascription may or may not be apt; still, most political activists know the dark night of the soul that is usually encountered as one engages in protest or action toward social change.

Following this, the Amabutho Male Chorus sings a stirring anthem *a cappella* in South African style. Entitled "America" with text rendered in Zulu, the piece is largely harmonized and employs some call-and-response as well as quite forceful rhythmic characteristics in the phrasing and accentuation of the text. An English translation reveals that now America is being called upon to hear South Africans' complaint and to lend support to their struggle. This text acknowledges the irony that while both countries endure oppression in different ways, both must work together, on different levels, to effect positive political change in South Africa. Within the "ritual" of this recording, this moment brings perhaps not catharsis or transformation, but certainly movement toward such an experience on the imaginative plane. Even without knowing what the literal translation of the text is, the choral sound and Zulu language embodies a strength of spirit that is irresistible and that etches a kind of inner portrait of a people whose ultimate freedom and dignity cannot be denied.

To conclude this musical event, the Art Ensemble presents a short and sweet, even gentle piece. A relaxed medium-swing feeling played by brushes is complemented by a broken-time bass vamp as polyphonic flute lines enter. A lyrical trumpet sound is heard once again, gradually giving way to an evocative soprano sax solo accompanied by bells. All three horns play just a wisp of a chorale-like phrase at the very end, but the final chord is very soft and disso-nant. The effect is as if to say, resolution may be at hand, but the process, the struggle must continue.

This is music very much oriented toward our time, one might say it is about a signal event of our time. The concept of the recording is overtly representative of the political and social issues addressed; the title, the narration, and the choral anthem are the emblems of this. But the musical structure and the fabric taken as a whole also arises from this concept, not as representation but as a presenta-tion of inner processes and dynamics fundamental to that concept. And even without the overt emblems, listeners should be able to sense something of the deep meaning of this artistic conception. Yet the emblems are not only helpful guides to our understanding, they are also integral to the larger musical event. Furthermore, the power of language, two languages in fact, is joined with the power of sound to evoke responses from us on many levels.

What I have been discussing in terms of the music of both John Coltrane and the Art Ensemble of Chicago is the notion that music may be heard as mean-ingful to its time, to our time. The starting points may be various, from an indi-vidual quest or from collective commitment. The approaches may be different, one reconfiguring musical elements and energies that resonated with larger social occurrences, the other creating new musical-ritual expressions that both repre-sent and embody cultural and political change. But they share an adventurous outlook and the ability to understand, hear, and play time as "all the time."

Further, these musics are superior examples of what Stuart Broomer meant when he said that improvised music "is itself a ceremony of freedom." For these musicians, and for many others, form and structure are not absent but rather undergo transformation or evolve in new ways to meet new demands. Some crit-icize the AEC for having become too structured and stylized in terms of its musi-cal-theatrical approach, and there may be some truth to that. Yet they remain masters of collective improvisation, that is, composition in the moment, even as their sense of preconceived structure has become more sure over the years, grow-ing out of their improvisations. With Coltrane's music, criticism was leveled at its seeming confusion and lack of structure, yet even at its wildest pitch, there was structure being evolved before our very ears. Moreover, the free play of imagina-tion in time opens up new possibilities for expression and celebrates human vitality and creativity.

Many of us simply do not know how to listen to these ceremonies of free-dom. Our urge for order, especially on familiar terms, dominates and forecloses on hearing these new possibilities. This means we may not hear the lineaments of creative, constructive new world visions being outlined or brought into for-mation. Believing we always need time to be measured and controlled, to be set in recognizable patterns, we may miss the multi-dimensionality of time itself, especially the flow of time that engages us in its process.

"Jazz time" in a more conventional sense, played by skilled performers, can give us glimpses of these possibilities, for it continues to be a profound source of illumination and enjoyment. Certainly refreshment of the spirit and a feeling of well-being is central to the jazz experience for all concerned. These are also attributes of the ceremonies of freedom that may be enacted in all jazz performance.

Still, for me, the pathway explored by Coltrane and further developed by groups such as the Art Ensemble of Chicago seems to speak most profoundly to our own time. These musicians have shown how music can be both entertaining and edifying while conjuring up other worlds of experience. Living amidst uncertain global political, social, and cultural patterns that also bear witness to hopeful trends, and privy to theories of our universe as dynamically expanding, yet seemingly governed by the uncertainty principle, we require music and art to be reflective of these new realities. In jazz, we need to acknowledge and celebrate those who are up to this challenge and whose musical creativity may indeed help us fathom our time more clearly. There can be room for nostalgia and comfort. But there must be space and time for the new.

SOME AESTHETIC SUGGESTIONS FOR A WORKING THEORY OF THE "UNDENIABLE GROOVE" | *How Do We Speak about Black Rhythm, Setting Text, and Composition?*

WILLIAM C. BANFIELD

> They always keep exquisite time and tune and no words seem hard for them to adapt to their tunes . . . so that they can sing a long meter tune without any difficulty . . . with the most perfect time and rarely without any discord.[1]
>
> Fanny Kemble, *Journal of a Life on a Georgia Plantation*, 1835

The unmistakable and most distinguishing art qualifier, or identifiable handle, of black musical artistry is its rhythmic complexity and vitality. Certainly there are many harmonic, sequential, or cadential conventions, licks and breaks that have been created by black artists in the African diaspora. But worldwide, and particularly within the last fifty years, black rhythmic conception has clearly dominated aesthetic conventions in popular forms of music. These conventions have had a major effect on music that has been composed throughout the world including traditional West African music, African pop, music of the Caribbean, and both South American and Latin American music. Reggae, and the African American creations in the states, the spirituals and blues, jazz forms (bebop, cool, and swing), rhythm and blues, funk, and certainly hip hop and rap forms have been shaped significantly by rhythmic conceptions. Also included in this family is the music of contemporary black American composers.

My aim is to speak as a composer offering suggestions on how to interpret black composed works from an aesthetic/cultural theoretical framework. I will do this by using some of Henry Louis Gates's literary observations, West African spiritual aesthetic sensibilities, and some African American notions of form, style, and feel. I tie all of these forms of expression to their common philosophical grounding: rhythmic expression. I am also trying to initiate a user-friendly aesthetic dialogue that attempts to speak about how one can talk about black rhythm and its vitality and how one goes about using "it" to create works of art as well. I hope to provide serviceable suggestions that can inform dialogue about the nature of contemporary black rhythm in both vocal and instrumental composed art forms. This dialogue will center around certain black-composed works and projects that have come about as the result of this "grappling" with the black rhythm aesthetic: T. J. Anderson's *Variations on a Theme by M. B. Tolson,* my own *Spiritual Songs for Tenor and Cello* and some reflections on Queen Latifah's *Black Reign* CD on Motown Records.

Henry Louis Gates, Jr., stated in *The Signifying Monkey* that "each tradition, at least implicitly, contains within it an argument for how it can be read."[2] If Gates's assumption is true, then there is no need to create any brand-new theory for how black art-making is done, how it should be perceived, or what constitutes its aesthetic life. Whether we are speaking of setting text to music, composing a new work within the stylistic families of black musical art, trying to get a handle on the meanings of its expressive power, simply talking about the artistic experience, the notion of "rhythmic life" is a primary issue.

I am defining *rhythm* as the science of coordinated movement in sound, but this extends outward to include all creative works, thought, and performance that comes with black art. This larger concept of "rhythmic life or life force" includes music, poetry, mythology, dance, and visual expressions of living (painting, sculpture). Black life and expression has RHYTHM. This used to bother me because it is exactly this idea that Europeans and white America would use to debase the intellectual and aesthetic value of black art and style, reducing black artistic quality to an innate ability to "keep good time." Rhythm, in my mind, means coordinated movement at many levels—physical, spiritual, symbolic, literal, and intellectual. I must return to my own "homeland" which is rich and fertile. I want to show evidence of this rich and fertile science, or life force, by examining its ideological roots and, as mentioned earlier, by examining musical examples in the literature that help to emphasize these points.

Ideological Roots and Paradigm Shifts

Duke Ellington once said of art, "It don't mean a thing if it ain't got that swing." Well, "that swing" is what I call the Undeniable Groove. The ideological and cultural roots of this rhythmic base are West African. A. M. Jones writes, "Rhythm is to Africa what harmony is to the European, and it is within the complex interweaving of contrasting rhythmic patterns that he finds his greatest aesthetic satisfaction."[3]

Western notions of rhythm in composed works define it as secondary or as a subordinate element that usually functions to link notes and harmony together. Time is followed and perceived to commence from the beginning at the start of a downbeat. African notions of rhythm are very different. This means that there is a completely different aesthetic viewpoint and meaning in place for perception, creation, and performance of artistic expression. John Miller Chernoff writes:

> Africans are concerned with sound and movement, space and time, the deepest modalities of perception. Foremost is the dynamic tension of the multiple rhythms and the cohesive power of their relationships. This involves the subtle perfection of rhythmic form through precision of performance, complexity and organization and control of gestural timing.[4]

Unlike a typical, classical seventeenth-century European order of musical design, in traditional black design, rhythm is the determining factor, the controlling element in composition or creative expression. Therefore, a paradigm shift away from Eurocentric notions of rhythm, form, text, setting, and performance practices needs to be recognized. We must resist the western idea that "existing monuments" form some ideal order that should then only be modified if acceptable to the canon and gravitate toward Hungarian composer Zoltan Kodály's belief that music should not be contrary to the natural melodic trend of a language. Again, each culture produces its own rules for the implementation of artistic structure. These rules work independently with, while critically "peepin,'" the old traditions to make sure they are in line with the new modes of thinking and living and creating art forms.

In Stravinsky's day, critics complained that he replaced the expressive power of harmony with motor power and argued that he destroyed sentiment and subjective emotions. In a sense, then, critics claimed that Stravinsky's art perpetuated a disdain for what was thought to be pleasing and beautiful. In a progressive black aesthetic, again on all levels, beauty is in the rhythm, the groove. The groove is moved to the forefront. This urgency of objective meaning in expression, and the immediacy of the perception of the direct aural experience, shifts us away from the European romantic paradigm. This "rude treatment" of expression, this urgency, this "soul" as some have called it, is what we mean by "life force" and vitality. This is now an aesthetic qualifier for artistic meaning.

Moving Toward Text and Double Meaning in Black Art

Another aesthetic suggestion and observation for black art in terms of dealing with literary forms, poetry, stories, myths, and love lyrics (blues, r&b), is, of course, its expressive liveliness in terms of rhythmic phrase construction (an issue to which I will return), but also its double face, or what Gates called "double-voiced"—essentially, black texts of being. These two aspects, rhythmic vitality and multiple meanings, are what gives black word-art forms their elasticity and depth.

The recognition of these art qualifiers is also essential to understanding the art and appreciating its power. Again, as Gates has suggested, they "enhance the readers experience of Black texts by identifying levels of meaning and expression that otherwise might remain mediated or buried beneath the surface . . . and suggest how richly textured and layered that literary artistry really is."

Black music has a long-standing tradition as an art form of rebellion and cultural creation, and these two characteristics are in many cases inseparable in the work. As Maya Angelou recently wrote of black poets:

> If African [blacks in the diaspora] poets have one theme, it is
> most assuredly the splendor of being Black. The poets revel in their
> Blackness. They plunge pink-palmed, black hands deep into blackness
> and ceremoniously drink the substance of their ancestry. . . . How can
> exaltation be wrenched from degradation? How can ecstasy be pulled
> out of the imprisonment of brutality? What can society's rejects find
> inside themselves to esteem?[5]

Many black works created in the African diaspora require the same inquiries. Furthermore, double meanings, codes of insurrection, and messages of spiritual freedom or political liberty characterize the depth of the black texts. This is also clearly illustrated in the following black spirituals:

"Many Thousand Gone"
No Mo auction block for me, no mo, no mo no mo
No mo drivers lash for me
No mo peck o' corn for me
Many thousand gone
"Steal Away"
Steal away, Steal away, steal away
I ain't got long to be here
"Swing Low"
Swing low sweet chariot, coming for to carry me home

In the past, musicologists might have dismissed these examples as simplistic, vacuous, and containing limited religious meaning. A more careful examination reveals that these songs are structured poetic texts with consciously constructed codes for insurrection and escape. Since the time of slavery, black ways of talking and expressing have caused these spirituals to become "coded private yet communal rituals." Upon hearing a spiritual, the blues, or modern rap, there is a reverberation of meaning, a duality that reveals there is always more than what the words say on the surface. This rhythm of meaning is another aspect that gives black art its peculiar value, what I call life force or vitality.

Esu-MC-Elegbara: The Mythological Cultural Root of the Rapper

As we consider the rhythmic vitality of black texts and this idea of the rhythm of meaning, we should consider one of the most compelling of newer forms of black expression, namely rap. In *Signifying Monkey*, Gates suggests that the middle passage did not obliterate significant artistic, political, nor metaphysical systems in black belief.[6] Gates identifies a mythical figure in West African culture, Esu-Elegbara, a double-voiced master of the spoken word, both spiritual and profane, a link between the gods and humanity. This figure was one who had the power of the spoken word, who became in his own conceit a trickster, a master of deceptive languages, a master of stylish expression. I offer another suggestion for the interpretation of black texts, and, in particular, the popular forms of the modern rapper: that somewhere, as Gates himself hints, there are vestiges of Esu-Elegbara within the expressive oral and written consciousness of black text writers. Black people in Cuba, Brazil, Miami, and Spanish Harlem all make references to this mythical character. Robert Farris Thompson, in *Flash of the Spirit,* has noted that Esu-Elegbara "became one of the most important images in the Black Atlantic world."[7]

Despite my own belief in the lack of artistic merit of many rap products, I can now see that the trickster, the gangsta, the hood-wearing, crotch-grabbing, hustling, jive-talking, double-meaning, self-titled poet, the lover of women/men, the slick, stylish, ego-bearing, macho-minded figure known as the rapper might very well be our old friend Esu-Elegbara in disguise. I am compelled by Gates's associations between black American literature and oral traditions to Esu-Elegbara. In terms of contemporary popular forms of text expression, we have to consider the power of rap music.

I am talking about traditions, styles, conventions, canon, and performance practices. In addition, I am suggesting that more consideration be given to the whole black experience, including the middle passage, and the cultural memory of African aesthetic values and performance practices to provide a foundation for performing, creating, and understanding black expressions in music. How do I take these suggestions and sample current literature to see whether these suggestions make sense for the contemporary composer and artist? What constitutes an appropriate understanding of black art forms that are composed and performed? By examining the comments and art of three creators, perhaps some of the suggestions for this dialogue will prove appropriate and applicable.

Text and Music

Composer T. J. Anderson states:

> I have always been interested in the result of music. It has been said that my approach to setting language is not traditional in terms of the way American and English composers set text. I see speech as rhythm. I mean that's what Black speech is all about. There is a certain vitality in language, particularly in Black speech and that's what I want to capture in my music.[8]

It is clear from this statement that the rhythm and vitality of black speech generates an aesthetic and, therefore, musical interest from which works of art have come. I have already suggested in my discussion of the values in other cultural expressions that different stress patterns in instrumental music as well as other artistic forms are many times derived from the treatment of speech patterns in vocal expression. The work that brings particular light to some of these aesthetic and cultural suggestions for examining black musical art works is *Variations on a Theme by M. B. Tolson* by T. J. Anderson. The work, composed in 1969, is scored for soprano, alto saxophone, trumpet, trombone, piano, violin, and cello. Its most intriguing and inventive aspect is its rhythmic invention. Second, it clearly stands firm in the traditional black-arts tradition, fusing spirituals, blues, bebop, and swing with European treatments of dissonance and Viennese notions of displacement of melody and *Sprechstimme*. Of note also is the use of double-voiced texts of African proverbs and a blues street text. The excerpt I want to focus on is Anderson's treatment of the blues text, which reads:

> Come back baby, come back.
> I need your gravy,
> I'm weak and wavy,
> Skidrowbound, talk of the town,
> and I don't mean maybe.

This lyric includes many elements of black literary criteria for black text and vernacular: slang ("baby"), metaphoric comparisons ("gravy" and sex), street rhyme, signifying (stating something humorous explicitly to mean something serious implicitly), and the duality of the bittersweetness in adult love relationships as heard in many blues lyrics. The final portion of the work is built on twelve-bar phrases like a blues structure, and the voice spins out lines in different permutations, lengthening and shortening words in all sorts of different rhythmic variations. This includes syllabic repetitions of portions of the text, creating a texture of motivic cells with the instruments.

In Anderson's work we have an example of a Western-schooled composer extending unique African American styles and traditions into the traditional European setting while simultaneously expanding the black traditions to include a European avant-garde aesthetic. The pitch organization of the work is generated from free associations and is heard in variations organized in motivic cells which are displaced pointillistically. These motivic variations are heard, in rapid succession, in ones, pairs, and groups of instruments, and then again in tutti explosions. Anderson constantly shifts his orchestration function from interdependence to solo, to voice against ensemble, in order to create a rhythmic texture that gives life to a seemingly hopeless and helpless plea in the text. The rhythmic variations and the interesting vocal treatment of the text, with half-spoken, half-sung glides, harsh rhythmic breaks in selected syllables, and rhythmically contrapuntal exchanges between the voice and the ensemble, are delightfully incomprehensible and are perhaps the most striking features of the work.

Variations on a Theme by M. B. Tolson is an unrecognized masterpiece in twentieth-century chamber vocal literature. The work stands firmly in the African American tradition as well as exemplifies the best in black style, conventions, aesthetic norms, and rhythmic vitality. (*See music excerpt 1 on page 42.*)

Spiritual Songs for Tenor and Cello

Spiritual Songs for Tenor and Cello is an example of the composer "revisiting the homeland" and recasting traditional African American spirituals in contemporary languages. The work has been criticized for "destroying traditional and sentimental religious values." It is simply a late-twentieth-century exploration of traditional black folklore, a reworking and recasting of music in order to explore the powerful potential of pain, despair, and the profundity of hope and eschatological vision inherent, but critically unexplored, in most spirituals.

The spirituals of black folk are some of the best examples of American folk philosophy, as profound as anything yet written. Over and above and under the adventurous treatment of music and text, and the profundity of depth and despair that fosters unshakable faith and joy, is the Undeniable Groove, which dresses the work and gives it its audible life force. A look at the text reveals literary aesthetic qualities such as duality, spiritual depth, and reflection as well as odd phrase structures that confound traditional text-meter configurations.

"Were You There"
Were you there when they crucified my lord?
Were you there when they nailed him to the tree?
Were you there when the sun refused to shine?
Oh, Oh, sometimes it causes me to tremble
Were you there when they crucified my Lord?

"Hold On"
Keep yo' han' on de plow, Hold on!
If you wanna get to heaven, let me tell you how
Jus' keep yo' hand on the gospel plow.
If that plow stays in yo' hand
It'll lan you straight in da promised land
Keep yo' hand on da plow and hold on.
Nora said, Ya lost yo' track,
Can't plow straight and keep looking back
Keep yo' hand on the plow and hold on
Mary had a golden chain,
Every link was in my Jesus' name
Keep on climin' don't you tire
Every rung goes higher and higher,
Keep yo' hand on the plow and hold on

Spiritual Songs for Tenor and Cello opens with the spiritual "Were You There?" In traditional settings, this piece is usually heard as a solemn hymn. Here, to the shock of the audience, it is cast in very dissonant, disruptive music. The tenor lines and cello accompaniment are set in non-tonal relationships, clearly dissonant, harking only referentially to the original melody and harmony.

There is the attempt to set up a painful and despair-filled landscape, ending in a very reflective and bitter cello cadence. Although another aspect of this piece is the slow rhythmic jar that is set up in the relationship between the two voices, clearly in "Hold On" the cello line is modeled after contemporary funk-groove bass lines such as those one might hear from Larry Graham or Marcus Miller. *(See music excerpts 2 and 3 on pages 43–45.)*

The rhythmic vitality both in the cello line and the tenor's treatment of the text and melody can be described as funk spiritual, if such a thing can exist. The entire vocal melody is not only disjunct and syncopated throughout, it is set in rhythmic counterpoint to a consistent backbeat in the cello line. This rhythmic texture projects a two-dimensional pulse where the notion of one and down beats are at times imperceptible. Then, midway into the composition, rhythmic characters of both instruments are reversed where the tenor voice is the anchor for the verse and the cello is cast in rhythmic syncopation against the tenor, off-setting the listener's sense of the downbeat. I illustrate the black rhythmic and philosophical concept I have been discussing by creating a musical landscape that says that even though the surface may be bumpy and the waters may roll rough, nevertheless, HOLD ON. The multiple meanings of spiritual reflection and social and political agitation and protest can be seen side by side. Even the social function of a piece of art such as "Hold On" has multiple uses and meanings and supports my understanding of the way rhythmic conceptions evolve in their totality in black art.

The New Popular Music Aesthetic:
Hip Hop Culture and The Queen's *Black Reign*

There are two main motives behind my investigation of hip hop. Besides the fact that it is clearly the most provocative musical art form of the last decade of the twentieth century, the real meaning of this new cultural activity is found among the "folks," where the operative meanings of language and behavior are used, created, and worked out daily. There are many social, political, and new postmodern aesthetics at work in "da hood," where urban youth breathe and work it out. Sociologically they are like the hippie generation of the sixties (rock and roll), or British youth of the seventies (punk, slam). The emergence of hip hop encompasses a paradigm shift wherein old notions of rhythm and black movement as the "simple-minded, natural behavior" of "negroes" is being broken. Rhythmic movement in this late-twentieth-century form is the self-conscious mode of intellectual and creative expression. Coupled with this fact is the need to tie hip hop cultural expression with all creative black expression within the diaspora. Despite its ugly commercialism and its sometimes harsh language, hip hop truly stands in the same camp as all other "welcomed" branches of the family of black-arts traditions. The emergence of new language forms (hip hop jargon) and modes of expression (in both music and movement, dance, and poetry) can be seen. Language, movement, and new aesthetic sensibilities create musical form, structure, syntax, and style. These elements are based on the "rhythmic way" in which another generation of young black people "speak." Again, the age-old question of the origins of music is answered.

For hip hop or rap music, I offer eight suggestions for operative modes of meaning:

1. The backbeat (or the Undeniable Groove), which consists of the dynamic tension of multiple rhythms and the unifying power of those relationships.
2. The Trickster Poet (Esu-Elegbara).
3. Gestural timing, or the Flow of the Rap.
4. The Message, including the coded play on language (signifyin').
5. Urban black self-renewal, life affirmation (postmodern secular spiritual empowerment).
6. New York and New Jersey tonality, language accents.
7. Covering, sampling, quoting, troping, speaking with other texts and musical grooves.
8. Communal affirmation.

Textual Analysis

While such great writers of black literature and critical theory as Zora Neale Hurston, Ralph Ellison, Langston Hughes, Lorraine Hansberry, Richard Wright, James Baldwin, LeRoi Jones (Amiri Baraka), Harold Cruse, Toni Morrison, and Maya Angelou might scoff at the following analysis, the work, "Listen 2 Me" by Queen Latifah[9] best illustrates many of the assertions I have made for literary, rhythmic, and musical meaning in contemporary, progressive popular black music today.

In this hip hop work, Queen Latifah plays out two roles I see in most rap, or hip hop, dramas. She is MC, Master of the event, making the party happen, dissin' and dimmin' on the rest of the "sorry-ass crews." She also functions as Esu-Elegbara, griot and rapper, bearer of cultural, social, and political truths because "hip-hip is for real." The main point of "Listen 2 Me" is this: "Aggravated youths" can always "know the time" (know themselves) if they would just "recognize the sign" (the emergence of the hip hop groove) and realize that no one can put a "padlock" on their minds. From the African notion that the spirit will descend with a good song—a form of postmodern spiritual secularism—each individual has the power to open his or her mind. The lyrics seem to suggest "Listen to me now" or, in other words, WAKE UP.

To many, this may seem simple-minded and vacuous, but to those within the cultural ritual, these meanings are premium in experience because they give life. The rhythm dictates worldview and taste, sensibility and values. The "sign" brings affirmation, self-worth, liberation, dignity in blackness, and new subcultural identity. The music, the beat, the "vibe," the message, the dance move, the rhyme, and the queen is here. Heyyyy! In hip hop culture, the rhythm, the flow, the flavor, and the style are, as with traditional West African cultural/ritual constructs, synonymous with God, the initiator of life. Even if the rappers don't know or acknowledge this themselves, they are trapped in the unavoidable web of cultural osmosis and transfer. Movement, then, is like God Spirit and represents vitality and life force.

There is an abundance of significant "handles," or hip hop terminologies, present in "Listen 2 Me."[10] Notions of double meanings, the importance and place of a philosophy of rhythm (or the flow) as essential ("you know that I can rock it"), the trickster-poet who is master of the spoken word, the rhyme, the flavor (style), and the reason, have considerable meaning and are all necessary ingredients for the people who are present in the song's scenario.

Conclusions

I have attempted to bring these works, concepts, suggestions, and assertions into a meaningful dialogue grounded in black aesthetic beliefs for intellectual creation of rhythm. By discussing these works and concepts within a specific cultural/theoretical framework, I wanted to illuminate rhythm's deeper and more meaningful aspects. These are aspects of rhythm that are often overlooked. Within the diaspora, black artists, philosophers, educators, intellectuals, poets, dancers, inventors, scientists, and singers have continued to forge meaning within multiple contexts of expression from blues poems to symphonies, from literary works to hip hop rhymes.

The key to understanding and appreciating these instances of beautiful expression is found within the arms of black creative expression. These works simply say: Touch me, embrace the rhythm of my expression and you will be moved by the sincerity of my motion, the depth of my emotion, the intelligence in my choices, and the spirit and voice of God in my convictions. Rhythm, the foundation of my being, is wide open to every kind of human expression. What I bring to you is the ultimate understanding . . . the Undeniable Groove.[11]

Music excerpt 1

Music excerpt 2

Music excerpt 3

keep your hand on the plough and hold on____. If that plough stays in your hand it'll take you___ to the prom - ised____ land____. Hold on

D.S. al Coda

Coda

Hold on____. Hold on

____> Hold on____. Hold on__

rit.

CHAPTER FOUR

RHYTHM AND RHYME IN RAP

ANGELA M. S. NELSON

Rhythm is the foundation of all African American popular and folk music. Rhythm in rap is especially important because it gives rap its movement, momentum, and a significant portion of its meaning. Since the art of rapping is based on a precise knowledge, skill, and ability to use complex rhythms, rappers themselves boast of their skill in being able to control it. For example, Public Enemy boasts in their rap entitled "Reggie Jax" that "homeboys and girls" will "testify" that "p-e-f-u-n and the K [Public Enemy *funk*, or music] will stay" and make their "body sway" because they have the "funky beat [rhythm] on the street" that compels their audience to dance.[1] The Jungle Brothers, hinting toward the religiosity of rhythm, say, "praise the rhythms,"[2] while A Tribe Called Quest recognizes the high importance of rhythm by simply calling one of their raps "Rhythm."[3] Female rapper MC Lyte wonders "why is it that your watch stops ticking but you keep clockin'?" and "no matter how hard you [try], you keep rockin'?" She replies: "Because I'm a 'slave 2 the rhythm'."[4] MC Lyte's experience suggests that rhythm is an "intoxicating" musical element, a ritual (to use an appropriate term) over which she has no control.

In "Revolutionary Generation," Public Enemy encourages the people to "just jam to let the rhythm run,"[5] as do female rappers Salt-n-Pepa.[6] When rhythm is allowed to "run," people will be compelled to dance and attain a degree of transcendent "communitas." As Cornel West articulates this in scholarly language, the "funky rhythms" of rap have a ritualistic (or religious) and cathartic function at black parties and dances.[7] The ritual involves being free (or liberated) at that moment. Rhythm that "runs" also has an aesthetic function for rappers—the aesthetic of soulfulness—and that aesthetic has a theology: soulfulness is of "ultimate concern" and is a means toward attaining transcendent distance for the unsoulful reality of racialist existence.

Rhythm is indeed highly valued by rappers, but, according to Kool Moe Dee and MC Lyte, so is rhyme. The majority of boasts in rap outline in detail the importance of giving a good rhyme, of the rapper being able to rhyme, and of the rhyme doing something spiritually (in terms of "soul") for its listeners. For instance, Kool Moe Dee, in his rap "Get the Picture," boasts that his rhymes are so extraordinary that "the gods will be packed in" (a club or auditorium) for him "to rock it" (which means to make such good rhymes and rhythms that the people are compelled to dance). Also, his rhymes are so "bad [good]" until "Aphrodite would freak as her knees get weak," "Zeus would get loose," and "Apollo's rhymes" would sound "like Mother Goose." Mercury would be "so hyped [excited]" that he would "spread the word" that there is a "dark-skinned brother in glasses [Kool Moe Dee]" who is the "new god of the mic."[8] Kool Moe Dee is obviously commenting on the power of his words, his *nommo*.

In "I Go to Work," Kool Moe Dee further boasts of his ability to rhyme. He says his rhymes are built as by an architect who constructs skyscrapers, and they are so "stupendous" that the minds of his listeners will be "trapped in his rap."[9] Again, his *nommo* is addictive: Once people hear his rhymes they will be forced to return for more spiritual empowerment. In "I'm Hittin' Hard," Kool Moe Dee continues to describe his rhymes and their effect on listeners. This boastful rap claims that even "skeptics" will be in his control because his "rhymes hold their minds in limbo," so much so that these subjects of his will "resemble a clone of Jim Jones" (the "spiritual" leader who demanded that his followers commit suicide with him because it was supposedly God's will). Kool Moe Dee "reprograms and deprograms about two million fans through rhythmic hypnosis." He leaves them in a "state of cataclysmic neurosis" brought on by the "narcotic known as rhyme."[10] I should say that this "narcotic known as rhyme" can in fact function as an "opiate of the masses" insofar as the achieved transcendence is cathartic. Whether the transcendence achieved in rap's ritual of rhythm functions existentially depends on the meaning conveyed in rap's texts.

The "cleansing" effect of perfected rhymes, or *nommo,* is illustrated in Ice Cream Tee's challenge to another MC: "My rhymes are a cleanser" and "I'll rinse ya."[11] MC Lyte's dynamic and generative rhymes are "always being taken by a sucker MC" who wants to be like her. Since she is the "master of creativity," other MC's want her power to convey ultimate concern effectively.[12] Queen Latifah makes it abundantly clear in "Come Into My House" that it is her "rap [rhyme] that rocks the party." In addition, she raps that "this is not an erotic interlude," nor an invitation for romance or sex, but a "rhythm call" for transcendence by an "Asiatic black woman" who has in the past and will continue in the future to "move multitudes" (impel her audience to dance).[13]

Too Nice, a rap duo, tells their listeners that they will "move their butts [impel them to dance] with just a rhyme on a twelve inch cut" (an LP recording). With confidence, they say it is "nothin' new because they have been doing these things for years." Their art is mastered so skillfully that they can "bust a rhyme like a bullet from a pistol."[14] Too Nice's claim of mastery touches on two important values in African American culture that also convey an urgency to transcend: spontaneity and skill (motility).

The cultural values of spontaneity and motility are connected to rappers' cultural contexts (code and symbols, verbal and nonverbal communicative behavior, and style). *Motility* includes factors like endurance and strength of movement. Motility is evidence of temperament and motivation. Other descriptives as defined by psychologist of music Carl Seashore include skill, precision, rapidity, steadiness, dexterity, and virtuosity. At best, motility can be understood as "a personal equation," meaning the unique and characteristic way in which a given individual can act (or perform). Carlton and Barbara Molette, in their Afrocentric discussion of motility, call it the "mastery of an art form." It is the exhibition of a high level of artistic accomplishment. Motility is important to African American audience participants because it lets them know that the performer has practiced often, well, and with sufficient discipline to master the necessary performance techniques.[15]

Motility enables black speakers to make credible presentations before African American audiences and to gain approval from those audiences. In rap music, the same motility must be present. Black audience participants respond favorably when "truth" is expressed. This truth-telling includes a certain skill in "expressing" the truth. Within the context of the party, rappers and deejays know that they have approval of their skill and performance style when their listeners collectively respond favorably, either verbally by yelling and screaming or nonverbally by dancing and "throwing hands in the air."

Spontaneity is highly valued in African American culture because (1) it exhibits a high level of artistic accomplishment and (2) spontaneous responses of both the performer and audience enhance the sense of community that is necessary in African American ritual.[16] In its purest form, improvisation does not appear in commercialized rap music.[17] However, in its performance the "improvisational quality"[18] of rap music is displayed when duos or groups of MC's perform raps in which they finish each other's lines, chime in and underscore one another, or simulate a conversation. In addition, even with this spontaneous behavior and improvisational quality, few MC's create substantial new material while performing. The fact is, rappers or MC's work out their "rhymes" on paper with some using a dictionary and thesaurus to expand their vocabulary.[19]

Spontaneity is also closely related to improvisation. In 1941, anthropologist Melville Herskovits noted in his unprecedented study of African and African American life and culture entitled *The Myth of the Negro Past* that improvisation was a device deeply rooted in African singing. He says that improvisation, especially in the African songs of recrimination (and the "dozens" of contemporary African American culture), was an effective mechanism for variation in diverse African musics and in developing individual style.[20]

Improvisation essentially mean to compose and perform simultaneously. Most improvised music is spontaneous, unrehearsed, and not notated beforehand. The vitality of jazz (held by some scholars to be America's only authentic classical music) is obtained from its spontaneity and originality. The significance of improvisation is that musical compositions are not carefully measured and fixed by Western musical notation and structure as in (nearly all) Western classical music.

Improvisation is highly valued in African American music because it allows freedom of artistic expression and spontaneity. Dwight Andrews illustrates the point of artistic freedom and spontaneity when he speaks of the use of rhythm in black music. He says the vitality of African American music comes from unequal divisions ("ruptures") of rhythmic pulses (as opposed to equally divided or sub-divided rhythmic pulses in Western classical music). For African American musicians who improvise when a rhythmic beat is already established, their challenge is to express their knowledge and understanding of the beat by *not* playing it. In other words, African American musicians show motility or skill by playing *around* the beat, instead of playing *on* the beat (as we see in Western classical music). Improvisation allows African American musicians to express themselves artistically and spontaneously, thereby illustrating their "mastery" or "power" over time by playing *against* time.[21] In sum, improvisation and spontaneity are necessary values in African American culture because they permit artistic freedom and expression of the African notion of "self-empowerment."

African Americans respond favorably to what they *perceive* and *believe* to be "truth." Molefi Asante says perceived logic or perceived facts are one major indicator for achieving spiritual harmony.[22] Therefore, in terms of improvisation, as long as African Americans *perceive* that African American rappers are spontaneous and improvisatory then that is the only criteria that should be evaluated. Despite the fact that, overall, rappers do not simultaneously compose and perform, as long as African American audience participants accept rap music as improvisational and spontaneous then we can agree that these concepts are indeed valued in rap.

Their masterful skill to "bust a rhyme like a bullet" actually speaks of the rap duo Too Nice's motility. Their rhyming ability is dependent first on a mastery of rhythm. In fact, rhythm and rhyme are closely related, as rappers themselves proclaim. Indeed, the term *rhyme,* for good reason, is a linguistic variant of *rhythm.* Rhyme is the "regular correspondence" of terminal sounds of words, lines, or verses, and rhythm is any kind of movement characterized by the "regular recurrence" of strong (long sounds) and weak (short sounds) elements. Rhyme, which uses vocal rhythm, is the most frequently used form of tonal semantics in African American discourse. Rhyme is found both in secular and sacred contexts. However, rhyme is most prevalent in secular discourse forms and it has come to be expected in secular discourse contexts of the artistic sort. In African American secular music, rhyme is evident in blues and especially in rap. Queen Latifah says:

> It's a new fusion I'm usin', (a)
> You ask what is it I'm doin'. (a)
> Hip-hop house, hip-house jazz, (b)
> With a little pizazz. (b)[23]

One of the key subjects rappers boast about is their ability to rhyme (just like the great rhymers did before them). Therefore, rhyme holds an especially central (and contextualizing) role in rap.

Rappers also use a technique that sounds like rhyming; it is "assonance." When verses are assonant, this means some "rhymes" are composed of words that "resemble" in sound, especially in vowel sounds. The accented vowel sounds correspond but the consonants differ, such as in this line from Public Enemy: "What you hear is *mine,* P.E., you know the *time.*" Rhymed or assonant verses are related to the cultural context of rappers. Their use of language will engage or disengage the audience. Therefore, the manner in which words are delivered, rhymed or assonant, is important to black audiences for the purpose of encouraging and sustaining "communitas," or the state of liberation.

As noted above, rhyme and rhythm are interrelated because they both involve the regularity of corresponding or recurrent sounds. When rappers use the right combination of words in their rhyming, audiences respond like they respond to good rhythms. As this process continues, rappers encourage a state of liberation and reconciliation (harmony and peace) akin to the situation described by Kool Moe Dee in his rap "I'm Hittin' Hard." Kool Moe Dee claims he transcends reality ("floats on his rhymes") and brings ("totes") the members of the black community ("loads and mounds of people") into spiritual harmony ("new heights") through his lyrics ("rhymes"). He is describing himself as an ancestral African shaman who, by rapping rhymes, is leading his people to a heightened form of community.[24] This is the achievement Philip Royster attributes to Hammer when he says "Hammer carries out the shamanic function of the santero—the person of wisdom in Santeria—by bringing the members of the black community into harmony with the energy, movement, and force of cosmic reality."[25] Kool Moe Dee, much like Hammer does through dancing, is identifying his shamanic role through rapping. They both are simultaneously leading their listeners to "communitas," to transcendence or a state of reconciliation and liberation (harmony, peace, and mental and spiritual freedom).

Although modern rappers often boast about rhyming, rhyme actually has a long and intriguing history in African American culture. Rhyme is generally recognized to be a basic ingredient of some forms of poetry (almost all forms of black poetry that have been popular), but linguist Geneva Smitherman says that the widespread use of rhyme in ordinary speech contexts is unique to black English speakers. Certainly this hints toward the inherent connection between rhyme and rhythm in the black aesthetic. Smitherman further notes that rhyme is used most frequently in secular discourse, although it has its own unique place in the sacred context when employed in a sermon, testimony, or welcome address.[26] An early example of the prevalence of rhyme in the secular discourse of African American culture is found in a song collected by folklorist Gates Thomas in 1891:

> Nought's a nought, figger's a figger,
> Figger for the white man, nought for the nigger.[27]

In his essay titled "The Blues as a Genre," folklorist Harry Oster notes the prevalence of rhyme in one of the principal musical forms of secular discourse. Oster reports that in blues with two, four, or variable numbers of lines, rhyme is a necessary element.[28] An excellent example is a blues titled "Eagle Ridin' Papa," recorded in 1929 by Georgia Tom of the Famous Hokum Boys:

Listen everybody from near and far
Don't cha want to know just who we are
Eagle ridin' papa from Tennessee
Now if you like the way we play
Listen chile we'll try to stay
Eagle ridin' papa from Tennessee . . .
We'll make you loose, we'll make you tight
Make you shimmy till broad daylight
Eagle ridin' papa from Tennessee . . .
I would never do brag, never do boast
Played this tune from coast to coast
Eagle ridin' papa from Tennessee . . .
Now if you like this tune, think it's fine
Set right down and drop a line
Eagle ridin' daddy from Tennessee . . .
Sometime we're down your way
We'll drop in and spend the day
Eagle ridin' daddy from Tennessee . . .
Now some want to know just what you got
Got good okra, man, serve it hot
Eagle ridin' papa from Tennessee
Now we ain't good-looking and we don't dress fine
The way we whip it it's a hanging crime
Eagle ridin' papa from Tennessee
If you see me stealing don't tell on me
Just stealing back to my ole used-to-be
We'll make you loose, we'll make you tight
Make you shimmy till broad daylight
Eagle ridin' papa from Tennessee.[29]

A contemporary example of the use of rhyme in secular black music is provided in a rap by Naughty by Nature:

That's what I do that's what I say that's what I live!
That's what I prove that's what I move that's what I give.[30]

Even at the dawn of the twenty-first century, the predominant secular context of rap music illustrates a strong preference for rhyme. The procedure of "making rhythm" and rhyming for rappers and most other black vocalists is as described here by the Molettes:

Words or phrases may be repeated several times in order to create a more rhythmic response from the audience participants. . . . A syllable, or even a whole word, may be omitted from a phrase if it interferes

with the rhythm pattern. . . . When black poets [or rappers] alter
the pronunciation of words, it is in order to make them conform to
a desired rhythmic pattern and not "'cause they can't speak good
English."[31]

In relationship to rhythm and rhyming, rappers also comment on the effects
of their rhymes and boast about how the rhymes promote a sense of group cohesion. Public Enemy illustrates this in "Fight the Power." In this song their peti-
tion is for black communities to wake up and revolutionize the social order—in
other words, become more ultimately concerned about their social and political
welfare. They promote a sense of group cohesion when they include the audience
by "calling" such phrases as "listen if you're missin' y'all," meaning that if the
audience participant misses Public Enemy's point, he or she should listen more
intently to the words. Overall, Public Enemy does believe their audiences are
actually listening to their message because they respond by dancing and screaming every time the group says "fight the powers that be."[32]

Other rappers have commented on how their rhymes unite the people
through the medium of dance, with the goal being the strengthening of group
gatherings and ultimately of the black community. The lead MC of Naughty by
Nature, Treach, says he is called the "wickedest man alive" because his rhymes
"make the people jump [dance]."[33] He also says he has a "new rap [rhyme] that
will put a dip [bodily movement] in the people's hips."[34] In other words, Treach
exemplifies the kind of *nommo* that will make people respond physically and
spiritually in a way similar to those who "shout" in the context of black religious
worship. In addition, Treach's knowledge of his own skillful use of *nommo* allows
him to boast that after he informs the people of what "O. P. P." means, he will
have them "jumpin, shoutin,' and singin' it."[35] Although the meaning of "O. P. P."
is strictly related to a secular concern (sexual activity), Naughty by Nature's pre-
ferred language—"jumpin,' shoutin,' and singin'"—is derived from a culture that
values the attainment of "communitas."

Kool Moe Dee causes his listeners to start "shakin' their heads" and "dancin'
instead of sittin,'" only "three seconds" after he puts in his audiocassette tape.[36]
Female rapper Yo-Yo receives adoration from her audiences because her rhymes
make them "move their hips."[37] Queen Latifah also illustrates her ability to unite
members of the black community. When her rhymes command that the people
"take a hand and throw it up in the air," those listeners not only obey her, she
says, but they also "dance for her."[38] In addition, the rap group Above the Law
has "the man with the plan [funky rhymes] to make the people dance,"[39] thereby
uniting black people through dance and strengthening the spiritual and physical
harmony of group gatherings.

Culturally speaking, African Americans appreciate rhythm and rhyme
because these musical entities help move the people to transcendence, a state of
reconciliation and liberation. This transcendence is like what drums have traditionally done for African worshipers. These have even greater impact when exe-

cuted with the aid of percussion instruments and the overall percussive approach to performance that is part of the black performance aesthetic.

In African American music, call-and-response patterns encourage and maintain spiritual harmony, a sense of group solidarity, and validate aesthetic and cultural values. African American musicians use several call-and-response techniques to accomplish these outcomes in addition to asking questions, making requests, and stating affirmations related to these outcomes. African American popular and folk musics, in general, utilize rhythms, a dominance of percussiveness, and call-and-response patterns to encourage the attainment of "soothing" transcendence, a state of reconciliation and liberation. Since transcendence is an "ultimate" goal, these elements are actually rituals that facilitate reaching that spiritual end. They are rituals because they are functional and formalized behaviors based on a group consensus.

The texture of African American popular and folk musics, or the rituals that make up the fundamental aesthetic of these musics, progress to the heart of what African Americans recognize as essential and important in their culture: reaching transcendent "communitas," thus enabling them to overcome their unique obstacles in America. This is what makes rhythm, percussiveness and collective participation through call-and-response theological: These rituals facilitate a state of transcendence for their listeners. However, above all, the basis upon which "communitas" occurs in rap (and, indeed, in all black music) is that "most perceptible and least material thing" called *rhythm*.[40]

CHAPTER FIVE

THE MUSIC OF MARTIN LUTHER KING, JR.

RICHARD LISCHER

Scholars of Martin Luther King, Jr., have long admired the richness of his rhetorical gifts. His grasp of metaphor, for example, enabled him to discern in local struggles for equal rights the eternal values of freedom, justice, and dignity. His was the prophet's gift of *seeing* the dignity of humanity in striking sanitation workers, the army of God in a peaceful march from Selma to Montgomery, and, of course, the kingdom of heaven in an ordinary meal at which white kids and black kids would sit together and treat one another like kin.

King was also a master of repetition in his preaching and public addresses. Repetition took many forms in his rhetoric:

Alliteration, the repetition of the first sound of several words in a line:

not . . . by the color of their skin but by the content of their character.[1]

Assonance, the repetition of similar vowel sounds followed by different consonants:

that mag-ni-ficent tril-ogy of dura-bil-ity.[2]

Anaphora (for which he is best known), the repetition of the same word or group of words at the beginning of successive clauses:

How long? Not long, because no lie can live forever
How long? Not long, because you still reap what you sow.
How long? Not long, because the arc of the moral universe is long,
but it bends toward justice.[3]

Epistrophe, the repetition of the same word or group of words at the ends of successive clauses:

In the midst of the howling, vicious, snarling police dogs,
I'm gonna still sing, We Shall Overcome.
In the midst of the chilly winds of adversity . . .
I'm gonna still say, We Shall Overcome.
In the midst of the bombing of our churches, and the burning of
our houses, I'm going to still sing, We Shall Overcome.[4]

In his use of repetition King always engaged in amplification, either by saying the same thing in so many different ways that it produced a cumulative effect or, more frequently, by subtly ratcheting up the value of the latter phrases in the series. His repetitions characteristically move up the ladder from the profane poets to the sacred writers or from examples in nature to examples in history. In his Holt Street Address at the beginning of the Montgomery campaign, his repetitions ascend from the ruling of a human court to the laws of Almighty God.

These and many other techniques of repetition are thematic in nature. They are dependent upon the content of the words themselves. The African American preacher and audience, however, also have at their disposal a second, non-discursive, track on which the sermon proceeds. This is the sermon's *sound track.*[5] Its meaning is as theologically rich as that of the theme track, but it is more readily available to experience than reason. King's reputation was that of a cerebral leader, a thinking activist. Anyone around him knew, however, that a significant portion of his message was conveyed on the sound track of his style.

The King sound depends on *rhythm*. Repetition is the father of rhythm in King's sermons, and rhythm is the mother of ecstasy. In the traditional religions of Africa, rhythm represents the most important modality of *nommo,* the word, for it is the source of the word's power and its capacity to give pleasure. We experience our daily lives as an interrelated series of repetitions. We eat, work, chat, tend our children, make love, sleep, and pray in predictable cycles of repetition. The *organization* of these for our well-being and enjoyment constitutes the rhythms of life. Rhythm is all-encompassing. Wyatt Tee Walker writes, "The same beat the Black folks dance to on Saturday night is the same beat they shout to on Sunday morning. . . . If you hear the beat and do not know what the program is, watch the direction of the shout; if the shout is up and down, it is religion; if it is from side to side, it is probably secular."[6]

King's sermons exhibit a masterful organization of repetition into rhythm. Strictly speaking, rhythm is not a sound, but the interval *between* sounds constituting their organizing principle. The sharper and more pronounced the consonants, the more clearly defined the interval between them and the more definitely established is the rhythm. Jon Michael Spencer notes that African Americans refer to this as "hitting a lick," which implies vocal percussiveness.[7] The repetition of alliterative consonants, multi-syllabic words or whole phrases, for example, "How long? / Not long," quickly establishes the excitement of the rhythm. King, like many musical preachers, often accompanies himself by rapping his knuckles on the side of the pulpit or on the Bible.

In addition to the repetition of sounds, words, and phrases, the predictable use of stress and pitch supports the sermon's rhythm. At regular intervals King will stress a syllable and dramatically raise its pitch and volume. When he moves into this vocal zone, his pattern of stress and pitch does not necessarily follow the *sense* of the words themselves. In the following example the underlining indicates a sharp rise in stress and pitch:

You can't *hem* him [mankind] in.
He has a *mind.*
Hold John Bunyan
In Bedford *jail*
He set there
But because he had a *mind*
His mind leaped *out* of the bars . . . [8]

Each phrase ascends by degrees to the peak of the accented word, which the speaker does not merely stress but *plays* or bends in a tonal curve. With sufficient repetitions King achieves a hypnotic power that is his to sustain or break.

One of the simplest enrichments of repetition is its alteration. He occasionally varies the pattern of stresses on the consonants and produces *syncopation,* which is a musical version of the black preacher's stylized *stammer* whereby he affects the Old Testament prophet's stuttering failure of speech when confronted with the divine will.[9] The preacher also uses the technique to signify a certain benevolent hesitation before dropping a bombshell on the congregation. The stammer says, in effect, "I, I, I really hate to say this, but I must." It also witnesses to the vulnerability of the gifted Afro-American preacher whose intellect may on occasion overwhelm an uneducated congregation. King uses the stammer frequently, producing an effect that cannot be duplicated on the printed page.

He also alters the pattern of his repetition by what might be called run-on rhythm. In his "Dream" speech, for example, he first establishes the rhythm with the repetition of "I have a dream," but in the third sentence introduced by that phrase he alters the rhythm by ending the sentence, "but by the content of their character I have a *dream* today!" He employs a similar technique in a sermon entitled "Guidelines for a Constructive Church." There he comes to a climax with an incredible eighteen consecutive sentences beginning with the phrase, "The acceptable year of the Lord is . . ." Between the seventeenth and the eighteenth he quotes the *Hallelujah Chorus* and cries "Hallelujah! Hallelujah!" Without a pause or a drop in pitch he adds, "The acceptable year of the Lord is God's year," the effect of which is to shatter his own rhythm. In poetic terms this is a run-on line or *enjambment.* Usually the resolution of the thought and meter occurs at the end of the line; run-on rhythm creates a sense of overflow of emotion. The speaker appears to be overcome with the significance of the "dream" or the "year of the Lord."[10] King uses this technique again in the fourth repetition of "I have a dream" and throughout his sermons and speeches.

While *stress* and *juncture* (or interval) help establish rhythm, *pitch* and *timbre* define the quality of the voice. King had a musical voice but, by most accounts, did not chant the climactic portions of his sermons as his father had before him and as many African American preachers do. A few of his friends, such as Wyatt Tee Walker, claim that he did "whoop" or "tune" or "moan" on rare occasions away from the glare of the media, while others such as Ralph David Abernathy, Bernard Lee, and Gardner Taylor insist that he never did. In a 1957 sermon he does say, "Preachers can't spend time learning to 'whoop' and 'holler' because they need to study so that we will know the gospel and can help people live right."[11] And in a later sermon he acknowledges the potential abuses of the sermon's soundtrack and indulges in some gentle self-mockery: In some churches "the pastor doesn't prepare any sermon to preach; he just depends on his voice, on volume not content. [laughter] And the people leave on Sunday and say, 'You know we have had a great service today, and the preacher just preached this morning!' And somebody says, 'What did he say?' 'I don't know what he said, but he *preached* this morning!'" [uproar].[12] There is no available recording of Martin Luther King whooping, but the gradual ascendancy of his pitch from a low growl at the beginning of the sermon to a piercing shout at the upper range of his high baritone, the predictable rhythm of the rise and fall of his voice, and the relentless increase in the *rate* of his speech, all contribute to the melodiousness, the song-like quality, of his voice.

Within a few minutes his voice moves from husky reflection to the peaks of ecstasy, but he always manages to keep both his voice and the ecstasy under control. Like a good singer he will open his mouth wide to hit the notes but will not reach or strain. His voice never breaks. Its power is such that even in the emotional climax of the sermons, King is usually not letting it out but reining it in. Had he been an incendiary, it would have been the other way around. On a very few occasions, however, King does lose himself in the conflagration of the response. In a mass meeting address in Birmingham, he concludes with nine consecutive sentences ending in the phrase, "We will still cry 'Freedom!'" As the listeners become ecstatic, King merges his voice with theirs and together he and his audience bring the speech to a frenzied climax:

> We will say Freedom, Freedom, Freedom, Freedom, Freedom,
> Freedom, Freedom, Freedom, to the world![13] [tumult]

King used the English language in a way that "remembered" his ancestral tongue. West African languages are tonal as is African American speech.[14] They convey meaning through the content of the words themselves, in the nuances of their pronunciation, and in the tonal qualities of the voice. Language takes on a melodiousness that allows an African American singer like Ray Charles to give the word *uh-huh* as many meanings as he chooses. The meaning of words like *uh-huh, yeah, Lord,* or *well* depends on the tone used in their inflection, which in turn depends on the context in which they are spoken or sung. A preacher like King may voice the word *Negro* (*Neg-ro, Neeg-ro, Nig-rah*) with the connotation that fits his point. Jon Michael Spencer compares African American preaching, including King's, to jazz performance, both of which improvise by vocal inflection. "Vocal inflections typically used by black preachers and jazz soloists include the bending and lowering (*blue notes*) of pitches, sliding from tone to tone (*glissando*), grace notes, fall-offs, and tremolo."[15]

The blue note, which is characteristic of the blues and black gospel music, recalls the middle pitch of West African tonal languages; it has a modality between sharp and flat that sounds sad to Western ears. When the preacher intensifies the message through a subtly crafted series of repetitions, or colors key words with bluesy intimations of irony, or renders the climax by tuning or chanting, he or she is synthesizing a "meaning" that transcends cognitive analysis.

In his sermon "Great . . . But," in which he argues that all human achievement is shadowed by failure and overshadowed by God's greatness, King pronounces the word *Lord* in such a way as to demonstrate the Almighty's majesty. *Law-ah-aw-awd* is a glissando. It begins on one note, curves around to two more, and returns to the original. Its very intonation witnesses to a God who is above all human greatness. In addition to these elements of musical style, King also produces a *turn,* which is taking a note slightly up and then partially down though not to its original note, or slightly down and then up but not to its original note:

> Through our airplanes, we've dwarfed *dis*-tance and placed
> time [*t-I-I-I-ahm*] in chains.[16]

As an indication of the intricacy of his vocal stylistics, in one sermon he does a *parallel turn,* which is two turns back to back in a syntactically parallel construction. Musical artists such as Aretha Franklin, James Cleveland, and Albert King are more closely associated with these vocal techniques than preachers, especially preachers like King, who do not "tune."[17] But these skills all belonged to King and are present in all of his sermons or speeches before an African American audience. Their use produces a *feeling* in the audience that offers the possibility of momentary transcendence of the suffering that has produced these blue notes and diminished chords in the first place.

Despite the abuse of his vocal instrument by cigarettes (a pack a day) and overuse (250 speeches a year), King easily ranged from huskiness to trumpet-like clarity. But the visceral response his voice invariably evoked was due to the quality of its natural vibrato. That suggestion of a quaver tells a tale of suffering and hope common to all African Americans. It tells the story of King's jailings and persecutions and thereby certifies his place at the front of the Movement. In the climax of "Great . . . But," he follows the standard practice of reciting a hymn verse in paraphrase, in this case, "Amazing Grace." A general tumult has broken out among his hearers at Ebenezer as the rhythm, range, and tremulous quality of his voice combine to exploit the full power of the stanza. At the line "I once was lost," the preacher roughs his voice like a jazz singer and interjects a throaty "*Yes I was.*" At that point, his identification with Jesus and the congregation is complete.

In the sermon "Great . . . But," the written word cannot adequately convey the pathos of King's voice. On its own track of meaning, the voice renders the story of deliverance. It is now ponderous and sad, then happy and defiant, next playful and filled with the wonder of human achievement ("Look at what we've done!"), then choked with the awareness of sin, and finally ecstatic with the hope of salvation—all within the space of twenty-two minutes. One senses that King's voice is only just managing to contain some overflow of suffering whose most natural expression might be a shriek or a chant. The dam is about to burst, wants to burst, but the preacher will not let it. Finally, when he cries, "I once was lost," and adds with a sigh, "Yes I was," that parenthetical admission grounds the old lost-and-found formula in the human frailty of the preacher, a frailty King may hide from everyone in the world but Ebenezer.

The vibrato is present in all King's preaching, as is the hint of his own frailty. The bluesy huskiness, however, appears only at the end of his career. It corresponds to the floundering fortunes of the Movement and his own worsening depression. Nowhere is the tonality of despair more evident than in the directions he gives for his own funeral in "The Drum Major Instinct."

> Yes, if you want to say that I was a drum major,
> Say that I was a drum major for justice [*Yes!*]
> Say that I was a drum major for peace;
> I was a drum major for righteousness . . .[18]

The preacher's imagination of his own funeral is an old device, but the pathos of King's voice, so perfectly attuned to the course of his own life, transcends all issues of style.

The key to any black preacher's style is the responsiveness of the congregation. The call-and-response pattern dates back to the West African ring shout and to the earliest forms of worship among African Americans. Call and response is a metaphor for the organic relationship of the individual to the group in the black church.[19] More specifically, the congregation's response helps establish the sermon's rhythm. While the preacher is catching a breath, the audience hits a lick on his or her behalf. Sometimes the preacher and the congregation are guided by an individual who acts as a "vocal coach" leading the responses. The coach may be a deacon or mother of the church; at Ebenezer Daddy King often filled the role with "Make it plain" or "Make it plain, M.L." One December evening in Albany, Georgia, King was invited to preach in the Shiloh Baptist Church where a great throng was gathered in preparation for a march. A reporter named Pat Watters remembers that as King's sermon reached its crescendo an old man punctuated each of his remarks with an authoritative *God Almighty*!

> How long will we have to suffer injustices? [*God Almighty!*]
> How long will justice be crucified and truth buried? [*God Almighty!*]
> But we shall overcome. [*Shall overcome,* the crowd choruses back]

King's voice, full of emotion that flowed into the crowd which poured it back to him, almost broke, shouting:

> Don't stop now. Keep moving.
> Walk together, children
> Don't you get weary.
> There's a great camp meeting coming . . .[20]

The response often provides the preacher a barometer by which to evaluate his or her performance: *"Preach, Doctor." "Come on up." "Yes." "Alright." "Only the gospel.*" "*Lord help him.*" Often preachers will ask or "beg" for it, not because they actually want an evaluation, but because they need the emotional encouragement in order to come up to the desired level, for if a vocal congregation is not moved, the preacher has failed.[21] The legendary Rev. C. L. Franklin begins a sermon, "I hope I can get somebody to pray with me tonight . . . because you know, I'm a *Negro* preacher, and I like to talk to people and have people talk *back* to me."[22] However stylized Franklin's request, it was a point of pride with King never to ask for help no matter how traditional the ritual might be. Yet he was no less dependent on the church's vocal response for his effectiveness than any local black preacher. To verify that dependence one has only to listen to the remarkably different effect when the same sermon is preached in a responsive church and a vocally unresponsive church. "The Three Dimensions of a Complete Life" preached at Mount Pisgah Missionary Baptist Church in Chicago and the version preached at Grace Cathedral, San Francisco, have eighty percent of their words in common—but they are different sermons. The responsive congregation appears to pump life into the speaker who, because of a brutal schedule, always sounds bone-tired. King drew rhetorical energy from lively audiences and in turn energized them in a unique way. In the African American church—and he preached the vast majority of his sermons in African American congregations— his message was accompanied first by encouragement, then exhilaration. In the many Shilohs, Friendships, Zion Hills, and Mount Pisgahs he managed to free himself of the heaviness of prepared notes and to preach the gospel of God's deliverance. He would come up, rise, soar, and hit the highest imaginable peaks of defiance, only to rise even higher to an extra-rhythmical exaltation of God or freedom, accompanied all the way by responses perfectly timed to his cries. On these occasions he would burn up the church. To vocally unresponsive congregations he preached the same manuscripts, but by the book and without the fire.

The congregation also helped King (and any black preacher) by completing his thought. On many occasions the congregation not only maintained the rhythm but rounded off Bible quotations and hymn verses for the preacher. In the sermon "Great . . . But," King has been building up the greatness of America in anticipation of condemning its sins. The congregation is in on this, so that when King cries, "America is a great nation," the word *but!* can be heard like little firecrackers going off, and one man succinctly finishes the thought, "*But she's goin' to hell.*"

The character of the response often follows lines of social stratification within and among black congregations. Some churches, like King's Dexter Avenue congregation, are what Evans Crawford calls "feel-back" (as opposed to "talk-back") churches where communication is accomplished through nods, smiles, and nudges. Bernard Lee notes that sometimes the response is delivered after the service. "Reverend, you were really in my pew this morning." Vocal response ranges from a dignified (if opaque) *well,* the meaning of which falls somewhere between a quizzical "interesting" to a downright *Amen* (not unheard in middle-class white congregations), to *My Lord, Thank you, Lord Jesus, Help yourself, Yes-sir,* and *Preach!* At the more demonstrative end of the spectrum one encounters loud laughing (*ha-ha-ha*), clapping, provocative sounds, and holy dancing. Even at Ebenezer, which falls squarely between a class-church and a mass-church, the response in King's day tended toward the conservative end of the spectrum.

Call and response signifies the communal nature of preaching and biblical interpretation. All are to some degree performers, and none are spectators, though the corporate performance in no way reduces the importance of the individual preacher's virtuosity. Call and response represents the congregation's love for its pastor and the pastor's gift to his or her people. By giving the people an important role in the praise of God, the preacher is reminding them of their importance as God's children.[23]

Repetition produces rhythm; rhythm is enriched by the emotional quality of the voice; and rhythm, feeling, and, finally, meaning are sustained by the manifold responses of the congregation. The final element in this cooperative venture is the sermon's climax or series of climactic moments, producing the final celebration. In King's sermons the climax is the "place" (in the classical sense of *topos*) where the *experience* of God replaces *talk about God.* It is the theological culmination of the address, but, stylistically, the climax also represents the most important rhythmic moment in the elevation of a black congregation. Any developed set piece will provide a climactic moment in the sermon. The preacher's rate will speed up significantly, and his voice will approach the outer limits of its pitch range and force. King's black-church sermons invariably contained several such climactic plateaus before the final ascent to the climax proper.

The true climax occurs within a few sentences of the end of the sermon. It builds upon the plateaus but contains material not found in them. Wyatt Tee Walker once asked his boss what his top priority was in planning a sermon— "your three points?" he asked. King replied, "Oh no. First I find my landing strip. It's terrible to be circling around up there without a place to land."[24] The climax is the celebration of the central theme of the whole sermon. From the announcement of its theme in the first sentence, a good sermon relentlessly circles its landing strip.

The climax restates the theme but in other media, sometimes by means of a hymn stanza or an ecstatic elaboration of points made earlier. This technique is what older preachers referred to as "making gravy." The material of the climax arises out of the rich, meaty ingredients of the sermon itself. The final climax may be built around a set piece, but the preacher's increased rate and run-on rhythms as well as King's extempore interjections and emotional outbursts will overwhelm mere symmetry of expression.

Finally, and most significantly, the climax will be *the* place in the sermon where the gospel of God is celebrated. Even in those sermons that have been heavy with moralism, advice, or admonition, King (in an African American church) will almost always find a place at the end for a celebration of the identity of God and the salvation of God's people. In "Great . . . But," for example, the only way the preacher can surmount the paradox of human achievement and human sin is by abandoning it to the mercy of God. In King's climaxes, like those of many black Baptist preachers, the solution is often expressed in terms of the speaker's personal witness:

> When I delve into the inner chambers of my own being, When I delve into the life of mankind, I don't end up saying with the Pharisee, 'I thank thee Lord that I'm *not* like other men,' but I end up saying, 'Lord [pronounced *Law-ah-aw-awd*] be *mer*-ciful to me a sinner.'
> [*Amen. Go ahead*! great excitement]
> And those sins that I'm able to escape I'm just thankful for. When I look at dope addicts, I just say to myself Law-ah- aw-awd, I'm thankful this morning . . .
> [*Yes Lord*!] . . .
> And, oh this morning, this is why I'm thankful to God. We must open our lives to him; let him work through Jesus Christ in our being. And he can remove that *but* from our lives.

To this he adds a moving recitation of "Amazing Grace," and abruptly concludes the sermon with the standard invitation to those who wish to come to the altar: "We open the doors of the church now."

The joy of style in King's sermons calls attention to the potential for conflict between pleasure and prophecy in all religious speech. In his comments on King's use of repetition, his biographer David L. Lewis was one of the first to question the social utility of the high style. Repetition was, of course, an essential ingredient in the King sound. With it he established a near-hypnotic rhythm by which he induced pleasure in the audience, won its assent, and, ideally, energized it for action in the community or nation. Lewis argues, however, that, far from energizing people for meaningful action, the pleasures of rhetoric dulled blacks to the experience of their own suffering and provided whites with little more than momentary emotional gratification. Like liturgical repetition, King's use of the technique engendered happy expectations of a ritual march or a pleasurable aesthetic sensation, but these turned out to be poor substitutes for real economic or social change.[25]

It is only fair to note that Lewis's comments were not made from the vantage of twenty years of black economic decline and disillusionment, but were published within two years of King's death while the battle was still raging. His criticism would be more telling if pleasure had been the only aim or achievement of King's style. But Lewis does not address the prior question, which is: What happens if no one *moves* the people in the first place? How are social forces peacefully set in motion? The critique of pleasure is mounted from the territory won by pleasure—and by two additional components in King's strategy of style: identification with the audience and confrontation with it. Beyond the beautiful words and rhythms, other rhetorical strategies would lead King to the fulfillment of his mission to America.

CHAPTER SIX

RHYTHM IN CLAUDE MCKAY'S "HARLEM DANCER"

RONALD DORRIS

Experiment and improvisation define the decade of the 1920s in American cultural and intellectual history. *Rhythm,* generally defined as measured motion, theoretically can be regarded as encompassing movement in both experiment and improvisation. Here we will focus on the sonnet "Harlem Dancer" by Claude McKay as an experiment in improvisation in order to assess the recurring patterns of speech, music, and biology that surface in McKay's composition.

"Harlem Dancer" is an Elizabethan sonnet. In the opening quatrain, meaning or experience is conveyed through the rhythm of words suggesting sounds. The words serve as a governing principle whereby the poet/speaker attempts to secure patterns in timing, spacing, accenting, and repetition that evolves and revolves.

> Applauding youths laughed with young prostitutes
> And watched her perfect, half-clothed body sway;
> Her voice was like the sound of blended flutes
> Blown by black players upon a picnic day[1]

The word *applauding* opens the poem and sets a tone of appreciation and merriment, not only in the first quatrain in relation to the rest of the composition, but also in relation to the title. Conceivably the applause is for the dancer in Harlem, whoever this may turn out to be. To *applaud* means to praise, approve, or commend. But one does not know who the accolades are directed toward.

Applause also means to show approval or enjoyment by clapping hands, cheering, and stamping, among other things. But no such movement accompanies the applause in "Harlem Dancer." Given the second word in the first line of the sonnet, one's gaze is directed toward applauding *youths.* Sliding down the scale of the remainder of the first line, we discover that the "applauding youths laughed with young prostitutes." Any impression that the youths were applauding the prostitutes with whom they laughed is quickly diminished by the shift in tempo from the plural youths and prostitutes in line one to the individual who appears in line two. One is aware that the applause and laughter succumb to observation. The individual who appears in line two is being *watched* by the applauding youths who laugh with young prostitutes.

Between line one and two of the first quatrain, rhythm is rearranged. The sense of action/motion conveyed by the words *applauding* and *laughed* have been subsumed by passive observers who *watched.* This rearrangement serves as a fulcrum that suggests, given so sudden a shift, that the poet/speaker's attitude in the sonnet is not aimed toward active/applauding/passive/laughed observers, but toward establishing the opening of the sonnet on a certain rhythmic note.

Keeping one's gaze focused on the opening word *applauding,* but searching for meaning in the root of the word, one hears the note that is being orchestrated. *Applaud* comes from the Latin word *applaudere,* which means not only to clap hands but also to strike. Apparently, the peculiar function of "Harlem Dancer" is to convey not sounds, but meaning or experience through words that connote sound. Had the poet/speaker presented corresponding motion with the applause—the clapping of hands, cheering, or a stamping of feet—such rhythm would have distracted attention from the poet/speaker's sense of striking a particular note. Hence the sound of applause without conjunctive motion is introduced not for its own sake, nor for mere decoration, but as a medium to suggest meaning. The function of *applauding* is not to steal the scene but to support whoever will later emerge on center stage.

Once the necessary note is struck, that vision is directed toward watching a perfect, "half-clothed body sway." Both in the rhythm of an actual dance(r) and the words that dance on the page, a new image is produced. However, the poet/speaker restrains the newness with additional words that convey sounds. What is perfect? The half-clothed, the body, or the sway? Just as one does not know from whence springs the rhythm of applause, one does not know from whence springs the rhythm of perfection or what is or is not to be perfected.

Because the poet/speaker is unable or chooses not to provide the audience with certainty about that which is *perfect,* he/she reverts to the use of metaphor. The voice of the dancer is like the sound of blended flutes. The word *blend* is derived from the Old English word *blendan* and the Old Norse word *blenda,* which means to mix. The Indo-European base *bhlendh* means to glimmer indistinctly, whence blind or blunder: to mix or mingle so as to produce a desired flavor, color, or grade, among other results; to mix or fuse thoroughly so that the parts merge and are no longer distinct.

The rhythm of blending in "Harlem Dancer" produces harmony. The voice of the dancer is not like the sound of any blended flutes heard any day, but "like the sound of blended flutes / Blown by black players upon a picnic day." The Middle English *blak* is derived from Old English *blaec,* which in turn is derived from *bhleg,* an Indo-European base. *Bhleg* means to burn or gleam, whence Latin *flagrare* means flame, burn; "sooted, smoke-black from flame." When the poet-speaker brings to the forefront a voice like the sound of blended flutes blown by black (the sum of all colors) players, a note of certainty is struck. Harmony progresses. The gleam that surfaces synchronizes the harmony of the dancer's voice with the laughter shared by the applauding youths with the young prostitutes. Playing out the *abab* rime[2] scheme of the first quatrain, an audience can join in the revelry to *tute* the *flutes* to *sway* the *day*.

Rather than have the quatrains in "Harlem Dancer" serve as a presentation of three examples of dance and the couplet as a conclusive statement addressing the collective strength or weakness of the examples, McKay establishes another arrangement. The quatrains suggest three metaphysical statements about dance as one idea—perfection, grace, and passion—and the couplet suggests the application of the dance to face and place. Throughout the sonnet a dance is taking place. For the dance to take place, there must be music. In the first quatrain, the rhythm of the music is produced by applause, laughter, sway, and a voice like the sound of blended flutes blown by black players upon a picnic day.

The extent to which rhythm unfolds in "Harlem Dancer" leads us to inquire about tone. In literature, *tone* may be defined as the writer's or speaker's attitude toward a subject, the audience, or him- or herself. In "Harlem Dancer" the poet/speaker does not project an attitude toward the applauding youths or the young prostitutes. He/she simply states that *youths* and *young* laughed with each other. The poet/speaker shows that the futility of expressing an attitude about a thing unto itself or about a fusion that is ageless (youths/young). The emotional meaning in the first quatrain does not issue forth from the poet/speaker but from the dancer. Like the sound of blended flutes, one hears the voice of the dancer.

By fingering the holes and keys along the length of a flute, the player produces high-pitched tones. The emotional meaning of the statement in the first quatrain is that all activity, all interaction, is high-pitched. Thus a voice like the sound of blended flutes serves as the *perfect* instrument to fuse the high-pitched laughter of applauding youths with young prostitutes. A voice like the sound of blended flutes is the perfect instrument to complement the *sway* of a half-clothed body. A voice like the sound of blended flutes is the perfect instrument to complement the high-pitched chatter that one imagines hearing on a picnic day. Rather than rely solely on the repetitious arrangement of words to register tone, the effective use of repetition as a musical device in "Harlem Dancer" surfaces in how a particular instrument can be accorded perfection if notes produced complementary parallel activity.

"Harlem Dancer" is also replete with biological rhythm. In the first quatrain there are applauding youths, young prostitutes, and a half-clothed body that sways, each possibly representing an imagined black player—or the imagined black player can be regarded as being separate from actual participants in the sonnet. Without the perfect instrument being tuned to complement such high-pitched activity, it is probable that each participant might compete to upstage the other were each poised to dance to a different tune. One is not allowed to see periodic occurrence of rhythm in specific physiological changes of the living organisms introduced in the sonnet. The rhythm of the sex life of neither the prostitutes, the youths, nor the dancer is revealed, nor are their sleeping and feeding habits revealed in response to a geographical factor (Harlem). What one sees is the periodic occurrence of the rhythm of an actual dancer or the rhythm of the arrangement of words on a page. Thus, blended instruments are utilized to complement the progression of the dance rather than the progression of non-focused periodic occurrence.

Just as blended flutes are a perfect complement to the high-pitched activity that synchronizes musical rhythms in "Harlem Dancer," they are perfect complements to biological rhythms. One meaning of *flute* is an ornamental groove in cloth or other materials. Thus it is conceivable that the half-clothed body of the dancer is replete with ornamental grooves. Given what becomes visible once a half-clothed body appears and sways, an audience can observe portions of the dancer's body without having to let the imagination wander and wonder.

Architecturally, a flute is a long, vertical, rounded groove in the shaft of a column. One can imagine that the motion of the individual in the first quatrain of "Harlem Dancer"—she bends, bumps, grinds and leaps into the wind—parallels the long, vertical, rounded groove in the shaft of a column. Thus the architectural image of a flute connotes the impression of a device that complements perfectly the biological rhythms in the poem. Among the applauding youths there may be boys who laughed with young prostitutes while they watched the half-clothed body of the swaying dancer. Hidden from view on what may be their fully-clothed bodies, these boys are endowed each with a long, vertical, rounded groove in the shaft of a column.

In the first quatrain of "Harlem Dancer," the dance is established and the perfect note is struck for the speech, music, and biological rhythms that will complement the dance. In the second quatrain, the measured motion of speech, music, and biology is fully clothed. Physical attributes that complement spiritual embodiment are brought to the forefront.

> She sang and danced on gracefully and calm
> The light gauze hanging loose about her form.
> To me she seemed a proudly-swaying palm
> Grown lovelier for passing through a storm.

Whereas quatrain one shows concern with perfection as the first metaphysical statement about dance, quatrain two shows concern for grace as the second metaphysical statement.

In quatrain one an audience is simply presented an impression of motion through a swaying body and the sound of a voice. The opening note of quatrain two reveals that impressions have given way to that which is concrete and therefore can be identified. The sound of the voice is a song and the sway is a dance. Now that impression is superseded by that which is concrete, the poet/speaker does not pass judgment but moves toward analysis. He/she accepts that the song and dance are executed "gracefully and calm." By foregoing impression for that which is concrete, what once was identified as half-clothed becomes materially endowed. Relative to the dancer, the half-clothes now are described as "light gauze hanging loose about her form." Whereas there is grace in the song and dance, there is no grace in the manner of dress that enshrouds the song and dance.

Given a graceful song and dance, there is no need for additional props to dress up these art forms, and such forms need not be overshadowed. As form, the song and dance should remain loose. To wrap these art forms in *gauze* is to endow them with too much structure. To fuel experimentation and improvisation, these forms should remain as fluid as the dancer. The French term *gaze,* probably derived from the Spanish *gasa* which in turn conceivably is derived from the Arabic *kazz,* means raw silk. *Gauze* is defined as any very thin, light, transparent loosely woven material of cotton or silk. Because the form of the dancer is wrapped in light gauze hanging loosely, there is the false appearance that her body and spirit are endowed with a transparency that the poet/speaker is able to penetrate.

The impression that the poet/speaker is able to penetrate the transparent body and spirit of the dancer rests on the shift from an objective tone in the first six lines to a subjective tone beginning with line seven. Thus all of the speech, music, and biological rhythms in quatrain one progress into the first two lines in quatrain two. The dance and song that accompany these rhythms are observed by the poet/speaker, but in the first six lines there is no admission of what the poet/speaker feels personally. In line seven of the sonnet, the poet/speaker turns inward to personal feelings, implying that the dancer may not be perceived by others as she is perceived by the poet/speaker. The poet/speaker simply does not see a body that sways but one that seemed a "proudly-swaying palm."

Some palms grow straight, reaching through the sunlight toward heaven. Others bend and lean as though weighed down by the burdens of some invisible force. The poet/speaker provides a safeguard to secure his/her subjective impression. What seemed to be a proudly-swaying palm is wrapped in gauze. Another meaning of *gauze* is a stiff material like thin wire. Yet another meaning of gauze is a thin mist. Here the sonnet evokes images of religious and nature symbolism. The light gauze hanging loose from the form of the dancer suggests an ethereal light that surrounds her body and spirit. As the dancer continuously raises her body in motion, the light gauze hanging loose about her form calls to mind the raising of Lazarus from the dead. The poet/speaker's impression of the dancer as a "proudly-swaying palm" calls to mind the season of Lent, particularly Palm Sunday. The season of Lent is a season of sacrifice.

As with quatrain one, repetition in quatrain two does not necessarily surface in the arrangement of words patterned to rime (although meter is sustained) but in an image that conveys a series of impressions along a continuum. But no sooner than familiarity with a particular idea is evoked, an abrupt change takes place. The final line of the second quatrain jolts us into a different focus. We are diverted from a focus on the power of religion to a focus on the power of nature. The dancer "seemed a proudly-swaying palm / Grown lovelier for passing through a storm." The storm is emblematic of both quiet and fury. Line four of the second quatrain bridges the tempo of the storm, as revealed in the first three lines of the second quatrain and all of the third quatrain.

It is conceivable that the storm that unfolds is a hurricane. Words such as *gracefully, calm, light gauze hanging loose, form,* and *proudly-swaying palm* connote registers in the tempo of a hurricane. It is conceivable that the dance, and the song that accompanies it, takes place in the eye of the hurricane. The eye is the center of a hurricane. Just outside the eye the full force of the hurricane is unleashed, at times extending several hundred miles in all directions. But within the eye, all is calm, skies are blue, sunshine is abundant, and the breeze just moves the palm so that is seems to sway proudly.

The measured motion of the dancer seems graceful within the eye of the storm. But once the eye shifts and the dancer is off center, she is confronted by the full fury of the storm. Quatrain three reveals that the scene changes from calm to an atmosphere that is dark and foreboding.

> Upon her neck black shiny curls
> Luxuriant fell; and tossing coins in praise
> The wine-flushed, bold-eyed boys, and even the girls,
> Devoured her shape with eager passionate gaze;

This quatrain opens with an announcement about the biological rhythm of tone relative to the "swarthy neck and black shiny curls" of the dancer. The announcement opening quatrain three suggests a *fugue*—a musical form or composition designed for a definite number of instruments or voices in which a subject is announced in one voice and then developed contrapuntally in strict order by each of the other voices. In quatrain three the poet/speaker, the key voice, announces the swarthy/black tone of the dancer. Contrapuntally, other voices develop the dancer as subject. The voice echo of tossing coins issues from the same source, the voice of praise that belongs to "The wine-flushed, bold-eyed boys, and even the girls" who, relative to the dancer, "Devoured her shape with eager passionate gaze." In turn, the same voice belongs to the applauding youths who earlier laughed with young prostitutes. This collective objective voice serves as the call that evokes a response from the dancer/subject, enabling her in turn to formulate a voice like the sound of blended flutes, black players, and the chatter of a picnic day.

The tempo of the storm motif parallels other shifts pertaining to tempo. In the first quatrain, observers *watched* a perfect body sway. When an area is under a hurricane watch, there is the possibility that the storm may move into that area. A certain sway in the breeze can indicate that the storm is brewing. The sway is a calm note. The tempo of a storm can be measured on the official Beaufort scale. Zero is the Beaufort number for a calm wind blowing less than one mile an hour. The tempo in "Harlem Dancer" progresses from a sway to calm. Momentum picks up to storm level, Beaufort number eleven, with winds clocked at from sixty-four to seventy-two miles an hour. Then tempo exceeds storm level, confirmed by a shift in observation from what is being "watched" to a "passionate gaze." To *gaze* means to stare, as in wonder or expectancy. Once a storm reaches hurricane proportion, one never knows what it will do next. The final number on the Beaufort scale, twelve, denotes hurricane winds blowing from seventy-three to a hundred an thirty-six miles an hour. The greatest hurricane winds can blow counter-clockwise from the eye at well over two hundred miles an hour.

"Harlem Dancer" is passionate; it's winds are constantly shifting. That is why the form of each quatrain is different. Only when all of the forms have been extended does the whole of the composition reveal itself. Quatrain one is like a sonata—an extended composition for one or two instruments consisting of from two to five movements related either by congruity or by contrast of tempo, key, mood or style, and sometimes theme. Some modern sonatas have single movements. The first quatrain in "Harlem Dancer" employs instruments of one design—blended flutes. The movements of these high-pitched wind instruments are likened to the voice of the dancer, virtuoso black players, and chatter on a picnic day. As the winds blow into the second quatrain, tempo shifts from the sonata to that cantata—a composition consisting of vocal solos or choruses, among other arrangement features, often with instrumental accompaniment, used as a setting for a story to be sung but not acted. Although a solo opens quatrain two, indicated by the word *sang,* as the eye of the storm shifts, the song does not retain emphasis; the shifting winds cause an alteration in form. In the very next breath, the shifting winds cause the song to be superseded by the dance. Whereas the sonata is sustained in all of quatrain one, the cantata is announced in the opening word of quatrain two but is not sustained beyond the announcement. Only in quatrain three, a fugue, is one able to see that the announcement in quatrain two is sustained transparently. By announcing the tone of the biological subject in one voice, the description serves as the whole that enables an audience to work through in reverse to determine that the subject is developed contrapuntally.

The final two lines of the sonnet, the couplet, are concerned with how to identify, register, or announce face in congruence with place or place in congruence with face relative to the perfection, grace, and passion of the dance(r). The face of the dancer is "falsely-smiling." Harlem, the place of the dance(r), is "strange." What is real and remains so throughout the composition is the communion feast that takes place among all the participants. The "wine-flushed," bold-eyed boys, and even the girls, "devour" the shape of the dancer. This blood and flesh ritual, eagerly and passionately consumed, is a timeless sustaining force that transcends all tempo shifts in the poem. The dance(r) is a collective force whose measured motion invites those who "watched" in the past and "gaze" in the present to partake in a communion feast in Harlem, a feast of life and involvement.

Apart from the Eucharist in the Western context the contest between face and place in "Harlem Dancer" calls to mind other contests, the age-old struggles between emotion and intellect and between time and place. Throughout the ages, in societies that live out a circular frame of reference as opposed to a linear one, to occupy space carries the threat of removal. Someone can come and pull a chair out from under you. But to occupy time and place is to live out an essence that nurtures an individual wherever he or she may be. In a circular frame of reference, time and place are internal and space external. Claude McKay's work shows a mastery of the craft of writing, but he was more concerned with social commentary than with the development of underlying themes structured around intricate symbols woven into experimental language. An exponent of the slice-of-life school, McKay wrote his own defense about what he attempted to achieve in his work.

> On the "broader" side (literally at least), my work has been approached by some discriminating critics as if I were a primitive stranger to civilization. Perhaps I myself unconsciously give that impression. However, I should not think it unnatural for a man to have a predilection for a civilization or culture other than he was born into. Whatever may be the criticism implied in my writing of Western civilization, I do not regard myself as a stranger but as a child of it, even though I may have become so by the comparatively recent process of grafting. I am as conscious of my new-world birthright as of my African origin, being aware of the one and its significance in my development as much as I feel the other emotionally.[3]

"Harlem Dancer" can be regarded as a slice-of-life statement that depicts social rhythms relative to internal and external movement among the first mass concentration of African Americans in one U.S. urban center. As suggested in the couplet, often they were falsely smiling faces in a strange place. Between the dawn of the twentieth century and World War I, African Americans moved in great numbers from the South to the North—many to Harlem. Relocation became their dance, and their voices, stories, and songs fueled the rhythms that became the dance's music. One person who contributed to the transformation in the lives of the new Harlemites of the twenties was James Reese Europe.

> The career of Big Jim Europe was a remarkable illustration of the fame and fortune then available to Afro-American performers. . . . In 1910 Europe incorporated the Clef Club, a combination musician's hangout, labor exchange, fraternity club, and concert hall. . . . Next came Europe's decisive role in a social revolution—dancing. "By the fall of 1913," Irene Castle remembered, "America had gone absolutely dance-mad." Still America was rapidly changing, and the Castles, Vernon and Irene, were leading the way. It was at this critical moment sometime in mid-1913, that Jim Europe, assisted by Ford Dabney, joined forces with the Castles.[4]

The concentration of so many African Americans in Harlem offered opportunities for businesspeople to package a "New Negro" movement. America, certainly New York, had a new urban enterprise that could be tapped into an ever-widening consumer market and culture. "Harlem Dancer" addresses much of the social underpinning of dance as consumer culture. Dancers were applauded as they swayed to jazz. Some forms of dance were graceful and light. One could loosely hang with certain steps, or kick up enough floorboards to give the impression of passing through a storm. There were those who tossed coins in praise of dance, drank wine in celebration of its contribution to culture, and passionately devoured it as an art form. McKay's assemblage in "Harlem Dancer" touches upon these activities.

The poem opens with applauding youths who laughed with young prostitutes as they witnessed the influx of the craze that was the dance of Harlem. Such applause surfaced on the heels of what once had been opposition. Before the dance craze took America by storm in the fall of 1913, there were those elsewhere and in Harlem who disapproved of its promotion.

> The moral spokespeople for the black community were as severely outraged by the dance craze as were those in the rest of Manhattan. "The Negro race is dancing itself to death," Adam Clayton Powell, Sr., said in 1914. "You can see the effect of the tango, the Chicago, the turkey trot, the Texas Tommy, and ragtime music not only in their conversations but in their movements and bodies about the home and on the street. Grace and modesty are becoming rare virtues." These virtues were very much on the mind of the *Age* two years later, when it commented on female entertainers who were "extremely careless about their attitudes and actions in dancing," and men who were "equally careless as to the character and nature of the songs they sang."[5]

A highly technocratic fast-paced consumer culture with a big-business ethic was causing a considerable rift in twenties America. More than ever before, sharp divisions were drawn between what was considered high culture, that dished out by the middle-class, and low culture, whittled from the folk. Experimentation and improvisation were the order of the day for proponents of both camps and for promoters who searched for ways to fuse the rift. America had emerged from World War I as a world power, but at the price of having to learn a valuable domestic lesson. A nation of immigrants had been horrified to learn that the first time they re-crossed the Atlantic en masse, they were returning to the lands of their descendants to annihilate them. Crying out against such injustice forced upon many of them by conscription, the land of golden opportunity took on the face of a strange place to scores of dissenters. America was not to forget the affront.

When the war was over, a new catch-all phrase—"making citizens alike forever"—became aligned with the process of Americanization designed to bring about mass conformity and uniformity from New York to San Francisco. The American populace was deluged and dazzled with the same silver-screen images, radio voices, and automobile ads from coast to coast. Dance played a major role in adding sameness yet contributing to the divisions being established in

American culture. This sense of duality was very pronounced in the rhythms of cabaret life.

> Like the movies, cabarets and nightclubs freed patrons from the restraints of work and home. They established a friendly environment in which informality, humor, and comradery [sic] prevailed, conveying an atmosphere of public sociability instead of public respectability. Ethnic entertainers . . . broke further barriers by sharing their vitality and spontaneity with patrons during and after performances. . . . Socially active college students frequently sought out illegal speakeasies to drink boot- liquor, rub elbows with the gangsters, dance to "hot" jazz combos, and pursue sexual adventure. Such temptation helped loosen the hold of the Progressive Purity Crusade and imbued the 1920s with their memorable label, the Jazz Age.[6]

"Harlem Dancer" presents self-expression and public displays of impulses that characterized both performers and audiences in twenties America. But the falsely smiling face of the dancer in a strange place alludes to an underlying horror. Despite democracy in motion brought on by dance, segregation was reality and legally would remain entrenched for the next thirty or more years. The dance scene was no exception.

> Blacks were happy to cash in on the white tourists, who were willing to spend their money on black exotica. Some Harlem nightspots so catered to their white clientele that they refused to admit blacks. The Cotton Club, on Lenox Avenue and 143rd Street, was for whites only, although light-skinned blacks could sometimes slip past the imposing doormen. The entertainment was all black, of course, although the famous chorus line featured "high yaller" dancers; a job in this chorus was so desirable and lucrative that it was rumored that white girls occasionally tried to pass for black in order to join its ranks.[7]

Dance contributed greatly to the American economy. McKay's reference to "tossing coins" in "Harlem Dancer" alludes to revenues generated by dance. The annual take for James Europe's incorporated Clef Club exceeded $100,000 during its best years. In March 1914 the Clef Club performed at Carnegie Hall. But unlike the entrepreneurial success of James Europe and the Castles, dance brought little or no profit to the masses in Harlem. For the masses, dance served as an art form that contributed to survival inseparable from economic necessity—paying the rent. To be allowed to dance in a club or a revue, or to throw a dance party, generally meant being able to pay the rent. The couplet in "Harlem Dancer" is succinct. Often the individual hosting the dance party and the individual living in the apartment, though one and the same, were different. "But looking at her falsely smiling face / I knew her self was not in that strange place."

These gatherings, originally conceived as a way to raise rent money, soon became a regular item in the social life of the ghetto working class. Brightly colored cards posted in the front windows of apartments announced the party. For the price of an inexpensive ticket, usually twenty-five cents, the party-goer gained admission to a stranger's apartment, where he found the rug rolled back for dancing, a piano for small combo in the corner, bootleg whiskey, fried fish, a steaming pot of chitlings for sale in the kitchen, and plenty of company.[8]

Africans in America have contributed to the shaping of this part of the hemisphere for the past four hundred years. In what would become the United States, international proprietors and domestic slaveholders sought those aspects of culture that would enable a capitalistic empire to be built. Despite camouflage or arguments to the contrary, it would have meant political and economic suicide to incorporate an unskilled and slovenly workforce to carve out the United States. Among the non-paid employees sold from auction block to auction block were those Africans most skilled in farming, animal breeding, dye and weaving functions, and crafts work. The rhythms of their lives and work produced music, and the music gave way to the rhythms of their coordinated motion in a strange place. When scores of these Africans came together in New York for the first time in what seemed an overwhelming urban setting, the synchronization of self-expression and private impulses revealed each participant/observer as the "Harlem Dancer" magnificently presented in a namesake composition. Claude McKay's sonnet serves as a lasting tribute to a people destined to survive in a strange place, and to the rhythms of speech, music, and biology that reinforce such struggle.

CHAPTER SEVEN

CHANTING DOWN BABYLON | *Three Rastafarian Dub Poets*

DARREN J. N. MIDDLETON

Introduction

Fortified by a mighty arsenal of word and rhythm power, the Jamaican singer-songwriter Bob Marley used his Rastafarian religious beliefs in an often bitter and protracted campaign against Christian missionary propaganda and capitalist imperialism. That was in the sixties and seventies. Since then, however, Rastafarian reggae and "dub poetry" has catapulted to the status of popularist art form. Today, an ever-increasing plethora of Afro-Caribbean poets are mixing their own Molotov cocktails of trenchant social commentary with militant, black liberation theology. Armed with potent lyrical grenades, contemporary Rastafarian "dub poets" are now launching their own Marley-inspired musical call to resistance. In this essay, I briefly examine the religious poetry of three such Rastafarian dub poets: Mikey Smith, Mutabaruka, and Benjamin Zephaniah. Possessed with intense focus and singular purpose, their nontraditional verse and unique rhythmic expression seeks to raise the consciousness of the hearer in a manner not unlike the Hebrew prophets and psalmists of ages ago.

The Way of the Black Messiah: The Roots of Rastafari

At the height of his powers in the late twenties, Marcus Garvey urged the poor underclass of a tiny Caribbean isle fervently to look to their African homeland for the imminent crowning of a king. Like some latter-day John the Baptist, Garvey and his "prophecy" helped to lay the foundation for the man who was to come and save the African diaspora from physical and mental slavery. And so, when Ras Tafari, son of Ras Makonem of Harar, finally was crowned in Ethiopia in the early thirties, black nationalists and influential preachers in Jamaica found new meaning in timeworn biblical verses. Of particular importance is Psalm 68:31: "Princes shall soon come out of Egypt; Ethiopia shall stretch forth her hand unto God. Behold Philistine and Tyre with Ethiopia: my son was born there." This, along with a host of other biblical verses, served only to confirm that Ethiopia had a special relationship with God. Not everyone agreed with this hermeneutic, however, for it appeared severely to anger those Christian missionaries and white colonialists intent on believing in Africa as the primitive, dark continent.

At his coronation, Ras Tafari took a number of theological titles to go along with others of a more regal nature: King of Kings and Lord of Lords, Elect of God, the Conquering Lion of the Tribe of Judah, and Power of the Trinity: Haile Selassie I. Terms such as these recall famous verses from the Christian New Testament Book of Revelation and, in one way or another, they were used in preacherly discourse by Leonard Howell, Joseph Hibbert, and Archibald Dunkley to "verify" Haile Selassie's divine status. In time, of course, early Rastafarian believers began to develop their credo to include the eschatological hope that Selassie I would help repatriate the black diaspora back to Ethiopia: the Black Man's Vine and Fig Tree.

Early Rastafarian preachment was enormously popular among the ghetto youth of Jamaica. A prototype of the liberation theology that is so vital in Latin America today, the Afrocentric thrust of Rastafarian beliefs initially provided much-needed hope and the possibility of improved life to a people long since marginalized and dispossessed by colonial rule. In the late thirties, then, Rastafarianism flourished throughout Jamaica with the force and veracity of a forest fire in summertime.

Since then, the mission field for Rastafarian preachers has extended beyond the boundaries of the crumbling and often violent projects of Western Kingston. Today, Rastafarianism is a worldwide phenomenon and is no longer confined to the lower socioeconomic classes.[1] In spite of this globalization, however, Rastafarian devotees continue to remember their humble roots. That is, contemporary Rastas continue to play an active part in Jamaican life by offering a social ministry for the poor. At the center of modern Rastafarianism, we could say, is an Africanized theology of hope for those caught up in a web of despondency: a Way of the Black Messiah. And nowhere is this ministerial vocation more dramatically worked out than in the lives of those Rastafarians dedicated to the use of language—revered today as a holy tool—to effect social and political *metanoia* in our time.

The Righteous Wail of the Soul:
Origins of "Dub Poetry" in Jamaica

Jamaica's native tongue is a unique form of Creole patois. This is an elusive dialect of English that owes a great deal both to African tribal vernacular and to the colonial plantation owners of the eighteenth and nineteenth centuries. One person stands out, however, as the pioneer of poetry written in patois ("dub poetry"). She is Louise Coverley Bennett, a.k.a. "Miss Lou." Originally educated at London's Royal Academy of Dramatic Arts in the early decades of this century, Miss Lou is credited with introducing a language often considered by colonial educators as too "uncouth" for "genuine" creative writing. To this day, however, she defends her use of patois with the claim that it was the "ordinary" discourse of the influential oral storytellers of her youth. That is, it was the life's blood of a people run down by centuries of systemic oppression or, better put, the natural linguistic mode for men and women who knew the liberating power of parable and story in a time of harsh enslavement. Here is a brief quotation from her famous poem "Back to Africa":

> Back to Africa Miss Matty?
> Yuh no know wa yuh dah sey?
> Yuh haffe come from some weh fus,
> Before yuh go back deh?[2]

Of course, Miss Lou's preference for the "language of the people" has its parallels in non-Jamaican writing as well. Consider Nikos Kazantzakis, the Cretan novelist, and his controversial use of the "demotic" form of modern Greek in his epic tome *Odyssey: A Modern Sequel*. Kazantzakis delights in the use of words and phrases familiar to the peasants of Greece—the fisherman and the coppersmith—but which are disconcertingly unfamiliar to the intelligentsia.

A similar reverence for the oral tradition—with its own special lexicon, strange spelling, and unfamiliar idiom—continues to be the chosen form of Rastafarian poets today. As a corollary, Rastafarian poets hardly ever pay attention either to grammar or established laws of poetry. There are some, like the poet U-Roy, who possess a keen eye for "grammatical correctness," but for the most part it proves very difficult to find a Rastafarian poem that is written in traditional meter (in English, the ten-syllable unrhymed iambic line of five beats)! Why is this? There are at least two reasons. First, the "educated" concern for "correct" language use in creative writing is viewed as far too stylized, restrictive, and oppressively Western. By contrast, Jamaican dialect is seen as vibrant, alive, and unable to sustain an interest in so-called "grammatical exactness"; it is the dub poets who have always known how best to create strong messages out of patois' unique and powerful word stock. Second, Rastafarian dub poets consider social conscience to be a more pressing concern than any zeal for the "educated" observance of "acceptable" literary form; it is the dub poets who have always worked hard to keep the conflagration of social resistance and community rebellion burning. In short, Rastafarian dub poetry is not a refined, classically aesthetic product. It chiefly is an evolving and dynamic grasping and re-grasping of the theological significance of current events. Mikey Smith, the dub poet whose work I will examine, puts it this way:

> We haffi really look into the whole thing of the language thing, because sometime it is used in a negative sense as a hindrance to your progress, and people think seh, "Boy, why don't you communicate in Standard English?" Standard English is good to be communicated, but you must also communicate in what you also comfortable in. And what is widely being used by your own people from which you draw these source. So that's why me communicate da way deh. And if me can really spend some time fi try to learn the Englishman language and so, the Englishman can spend some time fi learn wha me seh too, you know.[3]

Word Sound 'Ave Power: Mikey Smith and "Me Cyann Believe It"

A 1980 graduate of the Jamaican School of Drama, Michael "Mikey" Smith was born on September 14, 1954, and died on August 17, 1983. Until his mur-der—he was stoned by an angry and vicious mob in Stony Hill, St. Andrew, after a minor altercation—Smith was one of the truly outstanding and provocative dub poets in Jamaica. His performances, using reggae rhythm as a canvas on which to paint his social message-pictures, are still talked about with great enthu-siasm today. Here he explains how his fascination with dub poetry arose. Notice how enthusiastic he is to draw from the many uses to which patois dialect can be put by "ordinary" street folk:

> I was fascinated first by the storeman dem down at Orange Street.
> The man used to seh, "Come een, come een, come buy up, buy up.
> But no come een, come een, come tief up, tief up, cause we wi beat up,
> beat up!" A so them used to advertise them little thing, and me did just
> fascinated by that little rhythms, you know. And then me just feel seh
> me coulda do one too and do it better. So, you know, the whole thing
> start, and you just start to find different analogy. But dub poetry? Dub
> going to be the future, you know, a reggae music. A deh so it a go go.
> It a go dub-wise. It haffi go dub-wise.[4]

In a 1981 interview with Mervyn Morris, Smith underscores the claim I have been making thus far. Rastafarian poetry is an important pedagogical tool. Its purpose, in Smith's eyes, is to conscientize the hearer. That is, the Rastafarian poet's vocation is to raise the awareness of those whose senses have been dulled to the inequalities and rigors of life in Babylon—capitalist/imperialist society:

> I have fi really try fi educate a lot of people out inna earth,
> because, Jamaica how can it rest ya now, a whole heap of we can't read
> and write, you know. And we seem to rally round the spoken word
> very nice. . . . Poetry as a vehicle of giving hope. As a means of build-
> ing them awareness as such. Poetry is a part of the whole process of
> the whole liberation of the people.[5]

Smith's most famous poem is "Me Cyann Believe It." It is crafted around a phrase Smith would often hear repeated by ordinary folk in his Kingston community, and it is here used by Smith to chronicle the enormous struggle of the black Jamaican underclass in the face of the island's cultural, social, and political oppression. In the following lines, Smith offers an ironic twist on one of the many English nursery rhymes that the colonialists taught the slaves when they first came over:

> Room dem a rent
> me apply widin
> but as me go in
> cockroach rat an scorpion
> also come in

> . . . me naw go stdung pan igh wall
> like Humpty Dumpty
> me a face me reality.[6]

Written in a "blues mood" reminiscent of African American poet Langston Hughes, Michael Smith uses his poem to detail something of the squalor of the Kingston projects, together with the all-pervasive stench of hopelessness:

> Lawd
> me see some black bud
> livin inna one buildin
> but no rent no pay
> so dem cyaan stay
> Lawd
> de oppress an de dispossess
> cyaan get no res.[7]

And Smith, possessed with all of the righteous indignation of some modern-day Job, hurls his fury at a seemingly dispassionate God. In the following lines, the reader can clearly detect a note of heroic futility in Smith's theodicy. It is present, I believe, in his painfully honest supplication to the Lord ("Lawwwwwwwwwd"):

> Me seh me cyaan believe it
> me say me cyaan believe it
> Yuh believe it?
> How yu fi believe it
> when yuh laugh
> an yuh blind yuh eye to it?
> But me know yuh believe it
> Lawwwwwwwwwd
> me know yuh believe it.[8]

Bowing to no one ideology, Smith's poems nonetheless can be seen to espouse a worldview shaped by the benevolent philosophy of Rastafarianism. Although "Me Cyaan Believe It" makes no explicit reference to Rastafarian beliefs, others poems do, and Rastafarian fideism may profitably be extrapolated from some of the comments made in the Morris interview I have been drawing from: "Me is very close to Rasta, you know. Very, very close. In that a lot of things inna Rasta me can understand, and me can identify with. A that really make me very close."[9]

It is an incontrovertible fact that the world of dub poetry brutally was robbed of an immensely creative talent when Smith was murdered in 1983. Although the other two poets in this study subsequently may appear to be more self-consciously Rastafarian than Michael Smith, I think it is fair to say that he holds the honor of being the first "poet laureate" of the Rastafarian dub poetry movement, a highly decorated general in reggae music's call for moral revolution.

Jah Music: Mutabaruka as the Poet of Dread

The biting social themes covered by Smith in his verse were taken up by other writers along the way. By late 1983, critics in Jamaica began to say that the hour for the dub poet had arrived and that opportunities to effect social change were there for the taking. Writers like Oku Onuora and Linton Kwesi Johnson were among the first of a new batch of rebel poets, but it is to Mutabaruka that I now turn. An accomplished actor and song lyricist, Mutabaruka is a Jamaican writer driven by the concern to promote poetry as the instrument of social liberation and black consciousness-raising.

In "Nursery Rhyme Lament" Mutabaruka adopts Michael Smith's ironic use of colonial English nursery rhymes to drive home his perceptive social observations concerning life under Empire rule:

> first time
> jack & jill
> used to run up de hill everyday
> now dem get pipe . . . an
> water rate increase.[10]

And later still:

> jack sprat . . . ah, yes, jack sprat
> who couldn't stand fat; im start eat it now . . . but
> im son a vegetarian . . . 'cause
> meat scarce.
> little bo-peep who lost 'ar sheep . . . went out
> to look fe dem
> an find instead a politician . . . an
> is now livin in beverly hills.[11]

Mutabaruka closes the poem with a chilling reminder to the colonialists that long gone are the days when people could delight in teaching these and other famous rhymes to the "uneducated" masses. Human existence is far from the sugary sweet images of life made popular in nursery rhymes and Hallmark cards. In Mutabaruka's vision, everyday existence in the projects of Jamaica is excessively brutal for the brethren and sistren. Against the anti-realism of colonial nursery rhymes, then, Mutabaruka concludes this poem with his own lyrical call to arms:

> first time
> man use fe love dem
> but dis is not de time fe dem . . . cause
> dem deh days done
> . . . an wi write . . .[12]

Mutabaruka's Rastafarian theology is perhaps best expressed through "Say (for ODUN)." This is a brief poem, yet it provides an excellent example of how the Rastafarian poet seeks to transform the mind of the reader with its

Afrocentric pedagogy. In twenty short lines, Mutabaruka enumerates the essence of Rasta consciousness to include: (1) the belief in Ethiopia as the promised land for all Africans temporarily trapped in the West; (2) the importance of education in the fight to break off the shackles of mental slavery; (3) the need willfully to help topple all of Babylon's corrupt leaders from power; and, finally, (4) the belief that the essence of man is that he is divine. Here Mutabaruka's rhythmic verse recalls the intense Nyabingi drums of African tribal communities:

> when you remember home
> say:ETHIOPIA
> when you remember slaves
> say:BLACK
> when you shout revolution
> say:FREEMAN
> when you shout babylon
> say:DEATH
> when you speak of education
> say:GET IT
> when you speak of unity
> say:WADADA
> when you speak of God
> say:MAN
> when you see culture
> say:RELATIVE TO
> when you read all this
> say:MADNESSSSSS
> when you think like I
> say:RASTAFARI.[13]

The anti-Babylon polemics of "Say" are given a new twist in "The Outcry." In this latter poem, that is, Mutabaruka appears initially to impress on the reader a genuine sense of the utter futility of life in the West for the black man:

> leave west
> east best
> unite and fight
> sight
> JAH light . . . it right
> mighty might.[14]

With these lines, Mutabaruka seems to link himself with one of the central tenets of Rastafarian belief. That is, for the Rastaman the issue of salvation has always been tied inextricably to the theme of repatriation back to Africa. Even in their formative years, the Rastafarians doggedly resisted all forms of high-profile social involvement in Jamaican life. For this initial refusal to integrate, however, the early Rastas were heavily criticized by the media and orthodox ecclesiastical authorities. Even today, and with full knowledge that war-torn and ravaged Ethiopia is not the promised land of early Rastafarian preachment, a great many Rastas hold tenaciously to the eschatological hope of return to the Motherland. With "The Outcry," Mutabaruka appears confidently to locate himself at the heart of such Afrocentric theology.

Yet "The Outcry" seems to imply much more than this hope for spiritual renewal away from Western societies. In other lines, Mutabaruka appears to leave wide open the possibility of moral transformation, perhaps even in the most corrupt of political and societal organizations:

> to walk the streets paved with blood
> mud
> mixed with sweat and tears
> years
> of dreams to materialize
> wise
> man
> seekin new plan
> upsettin
> babylon
> gone above babylon infinity
> new martyrs found 'mong so-called madness
> of the city
> pity.[15]

Who can these "new martyrs" be? It is hard precisely to tell, of course, yet perhaps this phrase refers to how the emphasis of the early Rastas on "salvation as repatriation" has become less of an issue for a new generation concerned with helping emancipate the disenfranchised in their immediate sociocultural location? My research suggests that there may be a kernel of truth to this suggestion.[16] Contemporary Rastafarianism is an effective form of Caribbean liberation theology, and its current message of African identity within a Jamaican context has managed to comfort the poor, the oppressed, and the marginalized, who always have to be seen as the human material for the creation of new and just social orders. The "new martyrs" work in the madness of a decaying civilization, at least they do in Mutabaruka's vision, and it is they who strive tirelessly to "educate to emancipate" those whose senses are dulled to the inequalities and rigors of life in the West.

That the majority of ghetto youth require theological consciousness-raising in Jamaica is a tacit assumption in Mutabaruka's poetry. In "The Outcry," for instance, Mutabaruka seems to issue a passionate plea for Jamaicans to banish the missionary dogma that God exists in some otherworldly realm above the earth. Against this, Mutabaruka appears to assert the radical immanence of God within each and every man and woman:

Ras Tafari
herbs smell
tell
linkin man
to become one
why cry?
bring down from the sky
gods to die.[17]

The Rastafarian as assassin of the transcendent God! Mutabaruka's point here is central to the Rastafarian credo. And it may even be seen to be of a piece with Bob Marley's own realized eschatology, expressed so well in "Get Up Stand Up," the record that best summates the Rasta ethos, and which is almost "canonic" to Rastafarian believers and music critics alike.[18]

Finally, in "God is a Schizophrenic," Mutabaruka appears to honor this aspect of Marley's beliefs with his own self-consciously Rastafarian faith in the divinity of man and the redundancy of Christian missionary theology:

now all u religious people out there
I know u might not like what u hear
god in the sky
come down to die
god in the sky
a universal lie.[19]

One of the shapers of reggae dub poetry in the eighties and nineties, both as a singer and a producer, Mutabaruka does not appear to crave the publicity and hype that is commonly associated with the music industry. He prefers festivals and even makes a concerted effort to hold poetry workshops and seminars after his performances to teach his art and to encourage in others the life-engaging beliefs enshrined in it. Generally, Mutabaruka's corpus of writing seeks to relate Rastafarian theology to social engagement and to spiritual formation respectively. Disillusioned with society's fragmented and deeply unjust nature, Mutabaruka's verse is life-transforming preachment—a pedagogy for the liberation of black consciousness in today's world.

Capitalism in a Poetic Headlock:
The Dub Poetry of Benjamin Zephaniah

Although born in England, Benjamin Obadiah Iqbal Zephaniah spent the best part of his youth in Jamaica. His adolescent years, by all accounts, were traumatic and controversial. For example, he found himself taken out of his assigned comprehensive school at the tender age of twelve, largely because of discipline problems, and appeared then to have all the makings of an incorrigible ruffian. He arrived in London, however, at age twenty-two, and immediately set about writing verse for himself. Early books such as *Pen Rhythm* and *The*

Dread Affair were received with critical acclaim, and this in spite of the fact that he sees his role chiefly as a "performance poet" rather than one who works with the page in mind.

Zephaniah has toured throughout the world, earning himself rave reviews for the dramatic manner in which he delivers his verse, and at one stage was shortlisted for two prestigious writing posts: Creative Artist in Residence at the University of Cambridge, and Regius Professor of Poetry at the University of Oxford. Sadly, he was forced to endure malicious treatment at the hands of the British tabloid media during the selection process for both positions. That is, the so-called "gutter-press" in the United Kingdom seized on Zephaniah's "approved school" background, seeking to create a climate of fear in the minds of the selection committee, yet the press omitted to mention that Zephaniah has spent many years visiting schools, youth clubs, and teacher-training centers in order to hold workshops in creative writing.

Like that of the other two poets in this survey, Benjamin Zephaniah's Rastafarian poetry fits hand in glove with his political interests. In Great Britain, for example, he has served as chairperson of a number of housing and workers cooperatives, women's refuge centers, and theater groups. Not surprisingly, in his poetry he refuses to shy away from a rigorous and forthright analysis of the current British cultural scene. In "Dread John Counsel," he chronicles the slow, invidious decay of a political system that deprives black men and women of a genuine sense of identity and belonging:

> In this land my brothers and some sisters fight me down
> therefore in the dark place and the jailhouse I am found
> but I have a weapon that shall burn the enemy
> and it has a fallout that shall rule equality,
> the court is revolutionary the righteous ones shall stand
> and in the tabernacle there doth play a reggae band
> there is no House of Commons and everyone is high
> and this kingdom is governed by a upfull one called I,
> but I am here in exile so far away from home
> still in this sick captivity I will not use their comb.[20]

The comb reference requires some explanation. One of the most striking symbols of identity in the Rastafarian faith is the wearing of distinctive plaits or matted hair called dreadlocks. This brings to mind the Masai or Galla Warriors of Eastern Africa as well as the law in Leviticus 19:27. Rastafarians refuse to shave or cut their hair and, sometimes, will not use a comb either. The net result is that to see a gathering of Rastas is like witnessing the mighty and gracious movement of a pride of lions—primary symbol of African strength. Here Zephaniah's reference to "their comb" is a symbol for his trenchant moral resistance—itself inspired by Leviticus 19:27—to Babylon, and its many instruments of oppression:

we are not too fussy 'bout being British free
the kingdom's international a kingdom we can see,
they will never give us what we really earn
come our liberation and see the table turn,
still this is me in exile so far away from home
still recruiting soldiers to break this modern Rome.[21]

One controversial aspect of Rastafarian belief is the frequent use of marijuana as a holy herb. It is often referred to as the "weed of wisdom." This is
because of the legend that "ganja" purportedly was found on the grave of King
Solomon, and because "sinsemillia" is thought to assist the believer in times of
intense theological reflection, or "grounation" sessions. Rastas defend its use in
three other ways.

First, the Bible appears to support the smoking of herb. Consider Genesis
1:29, "And God said, 'Behold, I have given you every herb bearing seed, which
is upon the face of the earth, and every tree, in which is the fruit of a tree yield-
ing seed; to you it shall be for meat.'" In addition, Revelation 22:2 speaks of "the
leaves of the tree" that are for "the healing of the nations."

Second, this last verse underscores the general belief among Rastas that
ganja has an enormous calming effect on the consumer, reducing psychological
tension and helping the believer to acquire keenness of spiritual insight. The
"healing of the nations" reference is often used by Rastas to refer to ganja's proven
ability to assist in curing glaucoma and other illnesses.

Third, Rastas believe that ganja's functional purpose may be likened to the
use of incense and/or bread and wine in the Christian church. That is, it is an aid
to reflexive worship and sometimes takes on the quality of being a sacrament for
the pious devotee. The believer is not obliged to use ganja if he or she does not
wish to do so; rather, Rastas are encouraged to see its positive benefits and to
decide for themselves.

Benjamin Zephaniah versifies this particular aspect of Rastafarian theology
in his "Ganja Rock." That the holy herb inspires reflection ("third eyesight") is
clear from the first stanza:

Sip one time, sip two time
'til the mood is right,
hold a cool meditation
gain a third eyesight
as from time begun show your love for the sun
'cause as you burn you learn,
start from now for sure somehow
everyone must get their turn.[22]

Not surprisingly, the public or private use of marijuana still is outlawed in most
countries around the world. Against this practice, Zephaniah's "Ganja Rock" is
an explicit preachment to cultivate, nurture, and smoke your own weed—all in

the name of reverence for what nature supplies us with, and our own mental emancipation!

> lawmakers don't like ganja rock
> but if you look at the right clock
> I am sure you'll see it's ganja time,
> so liberate this ital weed
> it gives I headside vital feed
> and show them using herb is not no crime.[23]

As we have seen, the Christian New Testament Book of Revelation is often used by Rastafarians to "verify" many aspects of their theological beliefs. For instance, recall the connections between Haile Selassie's many regal titles and the apocalyptic figure of the Conquering Lion of the Tribe of Judah in Revelation 5:5, and the use of the "healing of the nations" reference in 22:2 to "support" the practice of smoking ganja in Rastafarian worship. In "Dread Eyesight," Zephaniah crafts a poem based on the Final Judgment by transposing some of the familiar images from the Book of Revelation. The notorious "four horsemen of the apocalypse" are now the "four dreadlocks" who arrive at the End Times bearing a banner on which is written Selassie's name and many titles.[24] And it is the "elders" of the faithful Rastafarian community who herald the closing of history with life-giving words of inestimable salvational value:

> We are the children of slaves and the victims of oppression, so
> from the land in which we are removed to let us shout with a voice
> that vibrates with dread and say to them men of earth, it is JAH
> RASTAFARI who giveth wisdom and understanding, for the land
> of Ethiopia has lifted up her heart, and the power of the trinity has
> opened the gates of Zion for the spirits of children who lived earth
> lives of great tribulation to enter therein.[25]

To close this brief account of Zephaniah's Rastafarian poetry, it is fitting to highlight one of the more important parallels between Smith, Mutabaruka, and Zephaniah: the Rastafarian belief in the divinity of every man and woman. For the Rastafarian, the spirit of Ras Tafari applies to all creation—rainfall, sunshine, etc. Yet is most fully incarnate in righteous men and women who abandon all belief that "God" is some supernatural reality "beyond them" and instead grasp the presence of Ras Tafari in all living things. In "Can't Keep a Good Dread Down," Zephaniah joins Smith and Mutabaruka in their theological immanentism:

> The Lion of Judah has prevailed
> the Seven Seals is I
> no living in the grave no more
> King Fari will not die,
> no brainwashed education

for wisdom must top rank
if you want riches
you must check Selassie I bank . . .
. . . Selassie I keeps on coming
can't keep a good dread down
those that stood start running
when JAH JAH comes to town,
greater love keeps coming
Alpha is here wid us,
so stop praying to polluted air
and give rasta your trust.[26]

These last two lines indicate Zephaniah's belief in the utter futility of praying to the Christian missionary God "up there," and is further proof of Rastafarianism's this-worldly nature. Finally, the line "King Fari will not die" must surely denote Zephaniah's outright rejection, as Western propaganda, of the reports of Haile Selassie's death in 1976. For Zephaniah, as for most Rastas, it is impossible for God, who holds the power of death in his hands, to suffer and die. And it is deeply incongruous for a holy man, a man who purportedly incarnated God Himself, to suffer the biblical "wages of sin." For Zephaniah as well as the other two poets in this brief study, Rastafari liveth!

Conclusion:
Dub Poets as Contemporary Psalmists

It is a well-known fact that the Rastafarian community does not possess anything like the Christian systematic theological tomes of either John Calvin, Friedrich Schleiermacher, or Karl Barth. They probably never will. In one sense, though, this need not prove to be a threat to the flourishing of their faith. On the contrary, the sure and inevitable decline of vibrant and dynamically evolving religious belief arguably occurs when believers busy themselves with the "central tenets" of their faith, and with the recording of these as numbered theses in weighty books! Against the propositionally oriented tradition of Christian theology, then, Rastafarianism has the distinct advantage of keeping what it believes "in solution" through the use of concrete images, metaphors, and parables. Like the psalmists of Hebrew antiquity, contemporary Rastafarians proffer spirited contextual wordscapes, imagistic litanies, and a sense of the holy eternally renewed in the common. Crying out against societal injustice and appealing for comprehensive urban renewal, the Rastafarian dub poets—especially the three I have examined in this essay—are modern, urban psalmists in a world seemingly unredeemed, paralyzed by hatred and violence. Michael Smith, Mutabaruka, and Benjamin Zephaniah—all three may be counted as Rastafarian liberation theologians on a spirit-driven, God-given mission to chant down Babylon!

CHAPTER EIGHT

RHYTHM AS MODALITY AND DISCOURSE IN DAUGHTERS OF THE DUST

D. SOYINI MADISON

Daughters of the Dust is the first film by a black female director to receive serious attention by critics and scholars, evoking passionate, albeit contradictory, responses by general audiences. While in the theaters the film "acquired cult status among black literati." By the time Julie Dash's *Daughters* was presented on Public Television's *American Playhouse* in September 1992, however, it was no longer written about in cult terms and was fast becoming an African American classic.[1] *Daughters* has won more than thirteen prizes, including the American Film Institute's Maya Deren Award and a Sundance Film Festival Award for cinematography.

Reactions to the film are varied—from beautiful to boring, from poignantly ethnographic to naively inauthentic, from postmodern to disjointed, from surreal to incoherent. *Daughters* is indeed enigmatic and provocative. However, despite the conflicting responses to the film, it is consistently heralded as eloquently revisionist and beautifully imaged in its representation of black women. The black female body is cast in a new light on the silver screen. Black women, especially, have sung praises to *Daughters* for displacing old and pervasive stereotypes of black female identity with more authentic and complex representations.

As black women, our sensors are heightened, but ironically accustomed, to seeing the traditional whore, mammy, lady, and superwoman on screen. Seldom are we seen engaged in cultural struggle and celebration. Instead we gaze too often at the whore—coupled with the lust and lasciviousness contained in the black bitch—who is cast less as a victim of destructive forces than destruction's embodiment and cause. Unlike the whore, the mammy is the eunuch matriarch: often jolly, bossy, overweight and overbearing and always taking care of other people's business. The lady—pristine, proper, and tightly controlled by grace, good manners and fine speech—is sharply contrasted to the whore and the mammy. The superwoman, a varied combination of powerful, sensual, beautiful, and relentless, is unconditionally adept at every task.

Contemporary representations of black women are a perverse admixture of the stereotypes of whore, mammy, lady, and superwoman or a combination of the neck-jerking sapphire and the Z snap B-girl. But representations not only project a subject together with how it has been historically treated, they reflect as well the culture that produces them. In this light, Stuart Hall's insight that the way a people are represented is the way they are treated becomes painfully relevant to the cinematic portrayal of black women. As we are bombarded with stereotypical representations of black women we are simultaneously looking at larger processes of racialization and patriarchy and how these forces are defined and positioned against the black female body.

Dash's film provides a brilliant glimpse of black women as symbol makers and cultural workers, as complex subjects and storytellers within a historical context. *Daughters* is a profound revisioning of black female identity because it evokes spiritual traditions built upon resistance, transition, and sisterhood even as it indicts those forces that have worked to constrain them. This revisioning, I will argue, is based upon a larger conceptualization of rhythm that must include rhythm as modality and rhythm as discourse.

Summary of the Film

According to Greg Tate, *Daughters of the Dust* is the "first translation of the sensibility found in contemporary black women's literature to the screen."[2] Dash states the influence of black women writers upon her work when she reveals how she:

> . . . stopped making documentaries after discovering Toni Morrison, Toni Cade Bambara, and Alice Walker in high school. I'd wondered, why can't we see movies like this? I realized I needed to learn how to make narrative movies. I couldn't believe it when I first read books like Toni Cade Bambara's *Gorilla, My Love*. I'd put the books down and say, "I know these people."[3]

In the film we find four generations of black women at the turn of the century (1902) on the Carolina Sea Island of Ibo Landing. From the narrative voice of an unborn child to the elder matriarch Nana, these women confront the tensions between modernity and the legacy of their African and slave past.

The story centers around one day in the lives of the Peazants, an extended African American clan whose slave descendants, isolated from the mainland, maintained a distinctive African American culture known as Gullah.[4]

Nana Peazant's grandson's wife, Eula, becomes pregnant shortly after she is raped by a white landowner. Nana calls on the ancestors and the spirit of Eula's unborn child to convince Eula's husband, Eli, that he is the child's true father, despite the rape and Eli's intense shame and anger. But it is not until the spirit of Eula's own mother comes to her that she is made aware of the spiritual presence of her unborn child. It is at the point when Eula embodies the spirits of both her mother and her daughter that she can tell the story of the Africans who walked on water to her unborn child. As she retells the myth to the unborn, spirit child, it is this story of the ancients and the power of the "old souls" that transforms Eli.

Through Eula's recounting of the myth Eli is now transformed and free to embrace both mother and child.

The second plot involves the clan's decision to migrate to the mainland against Nana's ardent opposition to them leaving the land that holds their history, the land that is the home of their ancestors. Before their departure, the family gathers for a reunion, a final picnic, where some family members—including Nana's daughter, the beautiful Yellow Mary—have come from far away. After living as a wet nurse and being forced into prostitution in Cuba, Yellow Mary stoically faces the insults and ostracism of the island women for being a "ruint" woman.

As the day draws to an end and the Peazants gather for the farewell feast, they are dressed in their finest. With the exception of Nana, the women mark the celebration with flowing white dresses and stunning, natural, African hair that is twisted, braided, dreaded, pinned, and cut in various styles. As the women prepare the food and assemble husbands, friends, and children for the ambrosia feat, the mood of the celebration is colored by a melancholy mixture of Nana's heavy-heartedness and the women's resentment of Yellow Mary. Haagar, Yellow Mary's cousin by marriage, is leading the women in deriding Yellow Mary while also voicing resentment of Nana's "hoodoo mess" and the ways of "salt-water Negroes." Haagar abhors life on the Island and is cruelly determined to move her family to the mainland. As one critic opined, "the gumbo simmers and so do family tensions."[5]

As the women complain about the old ways and taunt Yellow Mary, Eula steps forward and calls upon them to stop judging Yellow Mary and to love and honor the bond of black women. "If you love yourself," Eula declares, "then love Yellow Mary, because she's a part of you. Just like we're a part of our mothers." Eula continues her monologue and "pulls the mutters and shaded-eye whispers into a circle and argues for new standards for judging womanhood and selfhood."[6]

The film draws to an end as the Peazants mount the boat to leave for the mainland. Yellow Mary has decided to remain behind with Nana and Eula. Before leaving, Haagar's daughter, Iona, is "rescued" by her Native American lover, St. Julian Last Child. Galloping up to the barge, Iona runs to him and mounts his horse. As they ride off to live their lives on the Island, the camera then focuses on Haagar desperately crying out for Iona to come back, as relatives and loved ones console her as the boat pulls off.

The film ends with Yellow Mary, Nana, and Eula walking across the horizon with the image of the unborn child running behind them in slow motion. "While they are walking, each woman individually turns to dust and blows into the burning sun."[7] The unborn child declares, "We remained behind, growing older, wiser, stronger." The final image is of the unborn child alone, "along the horizon."[8]

Rhythm

One controversy surrounding *Daughters* is the narrative structure in which the story and images are framed. Some critics have praised it as a "nonlinear" form. In most of my discussions about the film with men and women, lettered and unlettered, viewers were both intrigued and disturbed by this. The montage of images that displaced the conventional beginning, middle, and end sequence was at certain levels both engaging and confusing. The viewers I spoke with felt their confusion was not rooted in a need to cling to order or linear sequencing. Rather their frustration grew from the attempt to connect beautiful, cinematic images where the relationship between them seemed, at times, incoherent. To these viewers and other critics, a more coherent flow of the scenes, in or out of order, might have more profoundly illuminated the meanings embedded within the film's symbols and images.

Another criticism of the film concerned its representation of Sea Island culture. Rather than view the film ethnographically, de Albuquerque suggests that we understand it mythopoeically. By arguing that black people on the Sea Islands in 1902 "did not go to the beach for picnic, nor did they frolic around in the sand dunes in their Sunday whites during the hottest month of the year,"[9] de Albuquerque frames his discussion of the film's other historical inaccuracies. First, he asserts that although *Daughters* is billed as a film in Gullah dialect, the majority of the major characters speak in various West Indian accents. Second, he charges that Ibo influence in slave history and the history of the Sea Islands is overblown:

> Ibo suicide is documented in the correspondence of slave mer-
> chants whose letters emphasized that Calabar (Ibo) slaves were to be
> avoided at all costs for they were "small limbed," "weak," "predisposed
> to suicide," and more likely to run away. It is not surprising that Ibos
> represented a very small percentage of African slaves in the Carolinas
> and Georgia. Ibo's only accounted for 1.8%.[10]

De Albuquerque asserts that there were various Indian tribes, including the Combahee, Stono, Etiwan, Hoya, Kussah, Ashepoo, Escamacu, and the Witcheaugh, but "there were never any Cherokees in the Sea Islands."[11]

These concerns around accuracy are important, if and when *Daughters* is marketed and represented as history. However, Dash is not promoting the film as a factual work, but as an imaginative construction reflecting a transcendent period of time in the lives of an African American family.

The discussions just outlined around the revisioning of black women as subjects on the screen, the claims of truth and accuracy within the slippery domains of ethnographic and ethnopoetic film, and the controversy around clarity of form and a nonlinear plot construction might evoke different responses and raise new questions if we experience the film less as a story that is unfolding and more as a reflection of rhythmic traditions where a ritual is evolving.

In interpreting *Daughters,* the concept of rhythm may be applied from two perspectives: rhythm as *modality* and rhythm as *discourse.*

Modality

Rhythm as modality involves order and patterned arrangements in time and space. Rhythm encompasses sound, movement, and image. In traditional West African cosmology, rhythm is the force that is at the root of all meaning and expression. It is the impetus behind the arrangement and ordering of all temporal manifestations. It gives form to our speech, our actions, and all of our creations. Senegalese author and Negritude proponent Leopold Senghor writes:

> Rhythm is the architecture of being, the inner dynamic that gives it form, the pure expression of the life force. Rhythm is the vibratory shock, the force which, through our sense, grips us at the root of our being. It is expressed through corporeal and sensual means; through lines, surfaces, colours, and volumes in architecture, sculpture or painting; through accents in poetry and music, through movement in the dance.[12]

Using Senghor's description that rhythm is "the inner dynamic" that gives being "form," rhythm is therefore both a motivation and a modality (in the West African sense) for artistic expression. Senghor further states that rhythm is evidenced in:

> the repetition, often at regular intervals, of a line, a colour, an outline, a geometrical figure, above all of our colour contrasts. In general the painter places brightly coloured figures against a dark background which creates space or intervals and gives the painting its depth. The drawing and colouring of the figures follow not so much appearances as the deeper rhythm of the objects.[13]

The "repetition," "the intervals," the ordering and patterned arrangements of colors, lines, and shapes against a background or space, according to Senghor is the essence of the work and is its "deeper rhythm."

In applying Senghor's concept of rhythm to the film, the focus is shifted to how certain elements, for example scenes, images, or symbolic actions, are rhythmically positioned in terms of visual patterns and relationships; order, repetition, and intervals give the work its design and form. The focus on rhythm as order, repetition, and intervals (this visual pattern within the art object's time and space) reverberates throughout black diaspora tradition. I will describe this phenomenon as rhythmic modality. This notion of rhythmic modality, as it specifically relates to *Daughters,* will be examined in more detail after a brief discussion of rhythm as discourse.

Discourse

Rhythm is a form of discourse because speech depends upon sound—that is, intonation, tempo, accentuation, cadence, and enunciation. These factors constitute the rhythmic words spoken. Africanist scholar Janheinz Jahn contends that "since 'man' controls things through the imperative of the word, rhythm is indispensable to the word: rhythm activates the word; it is its procreative component."[14] Senghor concurs, writing that only "rhythm gives it [the word] its effective fullness." In oral cultures and in traditional West African philosophy it is the word, "procreated" through rhythm that brings the world and all its elements into being. Existence does not precede the word, it is the word that precedes existence. Vietnamese filmmaker and writer Trinh T. Minh-ha states:

> African traditions conceive of speech as a gift of god and a force of creation. In *fulfulde,* the speech (haala) has the connotation of "giving strength," and by extension of "making material." Speech is the materialization, externalization, and internalization of the vibrations of forces. That is why, A. Hampate Ba noted, "every manifestation of a force is . . . to be regarded as its speech . . . everything in the universe speaks . . . if speech is strength, that is because it creates a bond of coming-and-going which generates movement and rhythm and therefore life and action."[15]

The connection between speech, rhythm, and life is manifest in the dynamic relationship between expression and experience. The idea experience organizes expression and not the other way around, gives expression form, and determines its direction.[16] If we concede that it is through the power of discourse—the word, speech, or expression—that existence and experience is ordered and made manifest, then it is rhythm (as "procreator" of speech as well as "generated" by speech) that helps determine the nature of existence and experience.

We may debate the intellectual and ideological grounding of Senghor and Hampate Ba's theories of rhythm; we may also justifiably criticize their privilege of expression over experience; and we may even chose to challenge the premise of rhythm as a visual ordering or as discourse. These assertions embody a fundamental belief system that spans West African traditions and oral cultures. Further, these conceptualizations of rhythm provide a means by which certain ambiguities within the film may be unveiled and clarified.

Daughters: Modality and Discourse

Richard Rogers writes, "Just as "subjugated knowledge" operates against and outside any particular discursive formation, there is more than one kind of rhythm—rhythms that discipline, control, reproduce an order, and rhythms that subvert, resist, and enact a different order."[17] Viewing rhythm as discourse and modality underscores the idea that rhythm extends beyond conventional notions of an aural, sensory experience—that is, as beats heard or performed through sound or music. As modality and discourse, rhythm is understood as manifestations of both form and content, seen and heard, encompassing deeper cultural implications that in varying ways reproduce or subvert social orders. Therefore, in *Daughters* a simultaneously unique and traditional social order, within an African American family experience, is presented within the film's frame through the discreetly varying rhythms of modality and discourse.

Rhythm as Modality

Rather than describe the composition of the film as nonlinear,[18] I would rather describe it as rhythmic. Sounds and images appropriated from black traditions are cinematically patterned and ordered so that at times they blend and at other times they contrast to create a rhythm of aural and visual sensations and meanings. Therefore, the "sights" and "sounds" within the frame form a rhythmic modality that underlies the structure of the film while reflecting patterns or themes within black culture. I see these patterns or themes (reflecting art and life) captured in three historical and cultural realms: the spiritual, the communal, and the individual. Within the spiritual realm, the film's focus is on ancestry and the unborn; within the communal sphere, the focus is on tradition and migration; and within the individual arena, the focus is on personhood as scorned and personhood as honored.

The fact that we perform certain rhythmic patterns in history and art is underscored as these three motifs reflect rhythms within the *real* existential time of black culture; they are elegantly appropriated by Dash as cinematic modality and discourse. They also show how rhythm "is a culture's means of identifying, differentiating, and relating objects, sensations, events, and processes in the world—whether artificial or natural, material or ideational, secular or spiritual."[19] In the realm of the spiritual, the ancestors and the unborn act as benevolent overseers for the characters. Ancestral spirits reign over the family as protectors and guides. "Their ancestors and ours all came through these Islands," Dash has stated.[20] Therefore, it is not the Greek gods that oversee their actions but the gods Oshun, Yansa, Yemoja, and Eshu-Legba.[21] Africanisms and ancestral traditions are woven into the many symbolic layers of the film, reflecting the people of Senegal, the Ivory Coast, and Madagascar. We recognize them from the Santeria high priestess[22] who sings sacred songs to Oshun, to the "drama of black hair."[23] It is this African past combined with the sounds and images of the unborn child that is a "transcendent mixed blessing of heritage"[24] and that is woven throughout the plot in rhythmic intervals.

The guidance of an ancestral past is reciprocally linked to the future of the unborn child for the survival of the present. Past and future narrate the present through the unborn child. This unborn child is the future, yet she is representative of the seed of generations past, of slavery and of freedom, of those who survived the land and of those who did not, and of the lineage of storytellers who bring continuity to the rituals of black life. The child is a metaphor for the boundlessness of time empowering thought and word to bring the story, to bring life, into being. The unborn child inherits the gift of thought and word before physical birth from the ancestors; without them she cannot tell the story. The sacred interplay of past spirits with future spirits within present time reveals an ecclesiastical process initiated to protect the continuity of life.

In the communal realm, rootedness and migration are reflected in the historical struggle around those who stay and those who leave. Leaving the island is symbolic of the "leavings" throughout the black diaspora. Leaving in the film illuminates a range of historical tensions. Leaving often meant departing from an environment connected to one's identity and a black past—an environment that provided the security and protection of ancestors, family, and tradition and where the symbols and rituals that help make us who we are were nurtured and safeguarded. Historically, the land was often felt to be an extension of our bodies. It was the land where the ancestors stood and worked. It was sustained under their labor and under their comings and goings. And, perhaps most importantly, the land is the place where they eternally rest. To leave the land was to abandon one's foundation, our root metaphor. The leaving in *Daughters* is a leaving reminiscent of leaving the south for the north, the rural for the urban, the known for the unknown—the community for the stranger. The film, however, does not simply and singularly lament leaving, it also graciously celebrates it. Dash understands that the rhythm of black tradition dictates that we must leave and we must stay. Some must stay to maintain the roots, to carry on the tradition, and to "feed the ancestors" with the birth of generations moving the land into the future. Others, however, must go to extend the lineage and the lessons of the land into more distant futures, to make change, and to impact a wider world.

In the realm of Personhood, the scorned and the honored, the film reflects the tensions between individual and communal identity and how one impacts the other. The film mirrors the universal theme of the scorned one as the disgraced and the honored one as the embraced. Dash illuminates the universal need for individuals to be part of a community and the consequences when there is a rupture between the two. Anthropologist Barbara Myerhoff states that "unless we exist in the eyes of others we come to doubt our own existence."[25] Dash depicts Personhood as inextricably linked to a community of others, who provide language, custom, belief, and nurturing for the physical, emotional, spiritual, and intellectual survival of the individual. The health and wholeness of the individual, predicated upon communal support, is presented as various themes throughout the diaspora. Dash balances the individual/community dynamic by establishing through the scorned and honored characters that community is reciprocally dependent upon individual thought, will, and action. As the women of the Peazant family attempt to scorn Yellow Mary and cast her as an outsider among their coterie, it is the voice of Eula that reminds them of the sacredness of an eternal sisterhood—a sisterhood defined by generations of mothers and daughters whose souls were infinitely bound together by history, land, struggle, and love and who live in flesh and spirit for themselves, their children, and their race. Eula's message is that power is a lineage of daughters born from a community of women who must know that if they love themselves they must love Yellow Mary, because she, like every black woman, is a sister and therefore a daughter of the dust. The spirits of these daughters are only as powerful as their collective love for each individual woman.

Rhythm as Discourse

Rhythm as discourse embraces Senghor's idea that "rhythm is the modality of the word" and that through language and the "word" we become known to ourselves and are transformed. This transformation where language is most profoundly linked with rhythm is exemplified in *Daughters* through a *ritual* unfolding of events. Since ritual in recent scholarship is primarily defined by the discipline out of which a particular discussion is grounded, I will clarify my use of the term in relationship to *Daughters*. Borrowing from anthropology and performance studies, I see rituals as encompassing these four descriptions: (1) rituals are performative acts having reference to beliefs in mystical beings, spiritual beings, or special powers;[26] (2) the ritual emphasizes "meaningful performance";[27] (3) the ritual embodies "transformative performance revealing major classifications, categories, and contradictions of cultural processes" thereby associated with "social transitions, unlike ceremony which is linked with social states";[28] and (4) rituals mark distinct phases within social processes, "whereby groups adjust to internal changes and adapt to their external environment.[29]

In viewing the film, the plot that unfolds before us can be most meaningfully described as a ritual. The focus, then, is less upon a form based on a nonlinear juxtaposition of scenes but on transcendence, social processes, and symbolic action enriched and propelled by rhythm and discourse. Understanding that rhythm constitutes order and patterns through time, we then understand that the performative acts, indeed the social acts, that comprise the ritual are part of a tradition where certain gestures and symbols have been reenacted or "repeated" across generations. That these gestures and symbols are culturally repetitive, shaping the meaning and form of the ritual, defines the nature of rhythm in ritual performances. Understanding that rhythm not only encompasses language and the "generative power of the word" but also gestures and symbols created and sustained by tradition, ritual is inseparable from discourse. James Paul Gee, describing discourse as more than language and literacy but as social practices, states:

> At any moment we are using language that we must say or write the right thing in the right way while playing the right social role and [appearing] to hold the right values, beliefs, and attitudes. Thus what is important is not language, and surely not grammar, but *saying [writing]—doing—being—valuing—believing combinations*. These combinations I call "Discourses" with a capital "D" ["discourse"]. Discourses are ways of being in the world; they are forms of life that integrate words, acts, values, beliefs, attitudes, and social identities as well as gestures, glances, body positions, and clothes.[30]

Using Gee's broader description of discourse, the performative framework of the ritual—language, symbol, value, body position, and gesture—are collectively understood as discourse. Therefore, the relationship between discourse, ritual, and rhythm may be understood by viewing discourse as the codes, symbols, or "languages"; ritual as the performance that frames, synthesizes, and communicates these elements; and rhythm as the force that orders and transmits these traditions or discourses.

In *Daughters,* the ritual begins with Nana evoking the generative power of the word through prayer. Her prayers are to the divine powers, the old souls who will send a spirit amongst the Peazant family to guide and order their path. Nana as elder matriarch and faithful believer is the interlocutor between the ancestral world and the existential present; she calls upon the spirit to come: "Come child, come!" The spirit, upon Nana's divine calling, is now welcome and arrives in the form of a child. It is the spirit child, assisted by myth and sacred rights, who brings clarity to the chaos of disbelief and disunity on the Island.

The ritual is now set in motion through Nana's calling and through the unborn spirit child. The spirit comes forth as the unborn child of downcast Eula and becomes the mystical manifestation of black women "who wear their scars like armor." As Nana calls upon the child, Eula calls upon the spirit of her mother, and in a dramatic moment they both are embodied within her, exemplifying Nana's words that "the ancestors and the womb . . . they're one, they're the same." The old souls and the new souls are but a continuum, directing truth and clarity as this cinematic ritual unfolds. It is the guiding power of the old and the new that will speak through Eula and will provide her with memory and story to continue the ritualistic transformation begun by Nana.

As the spirit grandmother and the spirit grandchild come together through Eula, the child is then set free to roam the island amongst the inhabitants and carry out the ritual of transition with Nana and Eula.

Eula enacts the next stage of the ritual as she recounts the Myth of Ibo Landing. Again the rhythmic forces of the old and the new—the continuum of past and future—is performed through Eula's telling of the myth. Eli, witnessing the telling of the myth and drawn to the spirit of the child, is then transformed; this is the moment when father is joined with mother and daughter.

The rhythm of black men and women fighting and dying and loving their way against the tumultuous history of lynching and rape is dramatically repeated in this moment through Eli and Eula. So is the rhythm of story and myth—memory and acts of resistance of those who came before—to teach us that we are "the fruit of an ancient tree."[31]

Eli now understands the "truth" but the ritual is not over for the "universal rite of passage"[32] is not complete. Nana, Eula, and the unborn child must join together to prepare the family for their journey to a new world. At the culminating point of the ritual, Nana with her talisman of ancient remnants speaks of *connections*—the "Root Revival of Love"—between the old souls and the new, between leaving and staying, and between memory and invention. She sets in ritualistic motion the rhythm of the diaspora that struggles past liminality to places of great possibilities, places to begin a new life where the old ways are preserved in story and deeds. There are those who cannot hear; they are distracted by distorted memories. It is Eula, possessed by the spirit of the unborn child and the spirit mother, who picks up Nana's tin can and says to the women:

> We're the daughters of those old dusty things Nana carries in her tin can . . . we carry too many scars from the past. Our past owns us. We wear scars like armor . . . for protection. Our mother's scars, our sister's scars, our daughter's scars. . . . Thick, hard, ugly scars that no one can pass through to ever hurt us again. Let's live our lives without living in the fold of old wounds.[33]

Nana holds up the talisman: "We've taken old gods and given them new names"; she places the talisman on the Bible: "This 'Hand' it's from me, from us, from them—the Ibo—just like all of you. . . . Come children, kiss this hand full of me." Field cries are heard through the Island as each family member comes forward to kiss the "Hand."

The ritual comes to a close as "The family takes communion from their great-grandmother, immersing themselves in their traditions and culture."[34]

They may now go on their journey.

Conclusion

Rhythmic modality is manifest through the arrangement and ordering of scenes and images. It is the mode in which symbolic acts and events are framed, and according to Senghor, the juxtaposition of symbols to "create space and intervals." Modality is characterized by artistic form and composition and serves as a channel in *Daughters* for subverting as well as reproducing certain social meanings and practices within and beyond the fictive world of film.

Rhythmic discourse is manifest through ritual. The ritual is the form by which discourse, "saying, doing, being, valuing, believing combinations," transforms reality and transcends experience. In the film, discourse, constitutive of a larger ritualistic processes, determines the destiny of the Peazant family. Certain rhythmic tensions within the diaspora are re-created and ritually performed, charged by the power of women and the African tradition.

CHAPTER NINE

RHYTHMS OF
RESISTANCE | *The Role of Freedom Song
in South Africa*

ALTON B. POLLARD III

Soweto is an acronym for South Western Townships; the name applies to the satellite settlement of black South African workers attached by an umbilicus of roads and railways to affluent white Johannesburg. Soweto is reportedly the largest city in Africa south of the Sahara, with a population numbering some three and a half million or more. The overwhelming majority live in impoverished conditions with little electricity or running water. Row upon row of tiny matchbox houses, so-called, crowd the unpaved and treeless streets.

It is dusk in Soweto. As far as the eye can see, smoke from coal-fired stoves spews forth; the air is thick with the pungent aroma of sulfur. Children and livestock mill about in the dirt streets, and women and men painstakingly tend to tiny garden patches. A small cloud of dust appears on the horizon as footsteps pound the earth to the cadence of the toyi-toyi, the traditional dance of protest and resistance. Someone has just died.

Relatives and friends squeeze together on rickety benches beneath a hastily assembled plastic awning, sheltering each other from the chilly winter night. Nearby, other mourners gather to whisper and to wait. The procession arrives, led by the cadre of Umkhonto we Sizwe ("Spear of the Nation"), more commonly known as MK, the military wing of the African National Congress. Dressed in combat fatigues, the young men and women of MK have come to pay tribute to one from among them who has fallen.

The vigil begins with fists and voices raised in solemn ceremonial song. It is the time-honored farewell to the freedom fighter, the "Hamba Khale" ("Go Well" or "Safe Journey"):

> Hamba kahle mkhonto.
> Wemkhonto
> Mkhonto wesizwe
> Thina bantu bomkhonto siz'misele
> Ukuwabulala
> Wona lamabhulu
> [Safe journey spear

Yes spear
Spear of the nation
We, the members of Umkhonto are determined
To kill
These Boers]

The language of the song is Xhosa, one of the most widely spoken languages in South Africa, the vernacular of the majority who are present.[1] The chant is melancholic and militant, a powerfully evocative mix of hymn and war song, protest and pain. The strains are deeply and fiercely insistent, a reflection of the brutally repressive conditions under which they are created. In the townships and rural areas, funeral music is resistance music, a ritual of the extraordinary in which the embattled human spirit is renewed through radically subversive song. The "Hamba Khale" is thus the first of many songs to be sung that night that are at once sacramental and regimental in mood.

Woza Jumbo
Hlala phezulu
Woza Jumbo
Hlal' emoyeni
Hlala phezulu
Hey masotsha
Hlala phezulu
[Say jumbo
Stay up there
Say jumbo
Stay in the air/sky
Stay up there
Hay soldiers
Stay up there]

The vigil of songs, chants, and slogans continues long into the night, in between emotional eulogies by family members, clergy, and comrades. Some songs exhort the mourners to answer the combatants' call to resistance, while others speak to the piercing pain of loss, especially maternal loss: "Mothers are going to weep, they're [government defense forces] going to fire a mortar at 7 A.M." Emphatic "yips" of ululation by women punctuate the night, as do cries of "viva," "amandla," and "mayibuye." An occasional "whoosh" from the crowd mimics the sound of mortar shells exploding. Finally, a twenty-one-gun salute thunders from AK-47s fired by the cadre of MK; others contribute the sounds of their own weapons. The funeral ends as the sounds of resistance fade. Dawn has arrived.

The Music of Resistance

Scenes like this one, reverberating with the sounds of sorrow, defiance, and liberation, are the bittersweet legacy of the struggle against apartheid. It is a drama that has been repeated countless times in open spaces, on small soccer fields and huge stadiums in black South Africa's protracted war against white oppression. Today, apartheid is officially dead and the African National Congress (ANC) heads a new government of national unity. Still, even with the advent of full democracy, radicalized forms of music, poetry, and dance—the rhythms of resistance—demonstrate their staying power. In this essay I will attempt to make critical sense of song as a revolutionary form of resistance in the anti-apartheid struggle.

What is resistance? As I define it, resistance refers to any form of social agency that holistically challenges human subjugation and oppression. Hermeneutically, the concept takes seriously the everyday quests of women, children, and men for personal dignity and self-respect beyond the expressly or overtly political. Resistance activity reminds us that human life is not solely defined by the extant political climate, whether "the struggle" is against apartheid, patriarchy, or economic injustice.[2] As my former colleague, feminist scholar Mary DeShazer, persuasively argues, "To define resistance solely as oppositional—for instance, as being powerless as opposed to possessing power—suggests that resisters are always victims and that struggles for a just society can be viewed only in terms of inverting the current paradigm."[3]

Resistance music plays a critical role in the mass democratic movement in South Africa. These songs are hardly monolithic in melody or message but often share the following features: (1) they are deeply rooted in the musical-poetic tradition of the indigenous peoples of South Africa; (2) they are folk expressions, composed, chanted, and sung collectively; (3) they offer counter-hegemonic models of peace, justice, and empowerment; and (4) they allow for improvisation to describe, explain, and map the currents of social change. I concur with D. K. Wilgus, who held that "truly national and popular poetry [or music] develops in a stage of society in which there is such a community of ideas and feelings that the whole people form one individual."[4] Indeed, the scope, sweep, and finesse of South African freedom song is broad based and revolutionary. Its lyrics are anonymous and recorded, traditionalist and modern, indigenous and Christian, and from Sotho, Xhosa, Zulu, Tswana, and more. Despite sweeping claims by whites to power and dreams of purity, Africans have struggled with life on their own terms, and made it sing.

"God Bless Africa"

From the very first moment the Europeans set foot on southern Africa's shores, attacks have been made on the indigenous cultures and traditions of African peoples. In 1497, the Portuguese explorer Vasco da Gama was reported to have been delighted to be received during his travels around Cape Horn by a group of Khoi musicians playing five flutes at a time. However, by the first semi-permanent occupation of the area by the Dutch in 1652, Europeans had come to realize that unless they were able to disrupt and disintegrate the African cultural fabric they would find it difficult to establish administrative and economic hegemony. Thus, from the advent of colonization, as famed South African jazz musician Jonas Gwangwa notes, "some folk songs, usually sung at funerals or in war, were either discouraged or banned."[5]

By the end of the nineteenth century, nearly all of the African population, predominately those who spoke Zulu and Xhosa, had been defeated either through war or diplomacy. In 1910, the descendants of Dutch and British colonizers agreed to form the Union of South Africa, effectively ending the European tribal war to control and dominate the region. Under this new white settlers' coalition the few rights blacks had were quickly eroded. Disenfranchised and dispossessed, a conference of African chiefs and leaders from across the country convened on January 8, 1912, to form the South African Native National Coalition, later renamed the African National Congress. One writer describes the opening of the conference in the most sacrosanct of terms:

> The Rev. Henry Ngcayiya, a teacher and leader of the Ethiopian Church, opened the dignified proceedings with a prayer. This was followed by an anthem composed for the conference by a Xhosa composer, Enoch Sontoga: *Nkosi Sikelel' I-Afrika*—"God Bless Africa"— was sung for the first time at a great African gathering.[6]

In truth, the composing of "Nkosi Sikelel' I-Africa" preceded the founding of the ANC by nearly twenty years. Its composer, Enoch Mankayi Sontoga, was a songwriter and teacher at one of the mission schools in Nancefield township near Johannesburg. Written in 1897, the hymn was first sung in public in 1899 to celebrate the ordination of an indigenous African, the Rev. M. Boweni, a Tsonga, to the Methodist ministry. According to South Africa's pioneer black historian D. D. T. Jabavu, "the composition was inspired by a depressed heart." Offering a social interpretation reminiscent of the creation of Negro spirituals in the United States, he writes, "black folk . . . were, at the time, far from happy, by reasons of straitened circumstances and because they felt they were not getting a square deal from the powers that be."[7] The first verse is well known:

Nkosi Sikelel' I-Africa
Maluphakanyisw' uphondo lwayo
Yizwa imithandazo yethu
Nkosi sikelela
Thina lusapho lwayo
(Woza moya) Woza woza
(Woza moya) Woza woza
Woza moya oyingewele
Nkosi sikelele
Thina lusapho lwayo
Morena boloka
Sechaba sahesu
Ofedise dintoa lematsoenyeho

(Oseboloke) Oseboloke
(Oseboloke morena) Oseboloke morena
Sechaba sahesu
Sechaba sa Afrika
Makube njalo
Makube njalo
Kude kube nguna phakade
Kude kube nguna phakade.
[Lord Bless Africa
Let her glory rise above
Hear our pleas and hear our prayers
Lord bless
Her sons and daughters
Come spirit
Come spirit
Come spirit, holy spirit
Lord bless
Her sons and daughters
Lord save our nation
Rid it of wars
and troubles
Save it
Save it
Our nation
Our nation of Africa
So let it be
So let it be

Thanks to the efforts of Zulu songwriter Reuben T. Caluza, "Nkosi Sikelel"
steadily gained recognition by the turn of the century. Sontoga had written only
one known verse, but Xhosa poet S. E. K. Mqhayi added seven more stanzas
devoted to such socially progressive themes as community, self-uplift, education,
and mutual understanding. Moreover, the hymn affirms that the singers and listeners are *Africans,* with a geographical and racial identity that is unitive beyond
the particularities of village, chiefdom, or ethnic tribe. Subtly, the song petitions
the holy spirit to intervene on the side of "Sechaba sa Afrika," the "Nation of
Africa," and against white domination. In 1925 the hymn became the official
anthem of the ANC. In the post-colonial period it has become the national
anthem of several African countries, including Zambia, Tanzania, Zimbabwe,
Namibia, and South Africa (along with the Afrikaner song "Die Stem").[8] For
many other Africans on the continent and in the diaspora it is the revered, if
unofficial, anthem of Africa.

At first glance, "Nkosi Sikelela" may seem a religious commonplace with its
appeals for divine intervention. I venture to suggest otherwise. A friend of mine

was in the United States recently to talk about conditions in pre- and post-apartheid South Africa. He recounted how blacks had persevered in their long, protracted, and determined confrontation with apartheid rule. He spoke about how women, children, and men had been unjustly detained, raped, beaten, and murdered by the police for participating in marches against parliament in protest against bannings of individuals and organizations. He referred to the imposed state of emergency on black townships that had once made it illegal even for church groups to hold vigils, light candles, or sing Christmas carols.

He then recalled a now-famous event that occurred on Tuesday morning, March 1, 1988. The world awoke to read in its morning newspapers about a mass march led by Archbishop Desmond Tutu and other members of the clergy. The group was first threatened with arrest and then fired at with a water cannon. A few began to chant "Nkosi Sikelela"; soon there was a veritable counteroffensive of song. Spontaneously and improvisationally, they called on the power of the divine to intervene on behalf of "Sechaba sa Jesu," the "Nation of Jesus." In the end, the performance of "Nkosi Sikelela" on that day spoke of the unity of struggle, of a determination to transcend differences of class and culture, ethnicity, and gender, in the all-embracing quest for freedom. It is hardly an accident that the state apparatus tried for the last thirty years of apartheid and under various regimes to appropriate the song. For the irrefutable facts are that those who resisted apartheid—multiethnic, male and female, sometimes secularized, always determined—continually turned political oppression to political advantage via the idiom of African sacred song.

Prior to the forties the ANC's campaign against state suppression was largely conducted through petitions, representations, and delegations to the government. Not civil disobedience, which was yet to be learned from the Indian community, but civilized protest was the formative strategy. Invoking the "ideals of Christianity, human decency, and democracy," leaders of the movement sought a moral hearing for South Africa's black population.[9] Although the ANC exposed a profound paradox in the policies of a self-professed Christian government, its call for a true Christian civilization resulted in no tangible redress of African grievances.

During the next few years the ANC metamorphosed beyond being an elite, mission-educated vanguard to become a diffuse political movement of students, church people, teachers, nurses, artisans, lawyers, domestic workers, social workers, journalists, physicians, and unionists. A signal indication of the new activism was the formation in 1944 of the Congress Youth League (CYL). The Youth League's leader, Anton Lembede, espoused a militant nationalism that was to be enshrined in the phrase "Africa for Africans, Africans for humanity, and humanity for God and Africa." Lembede's fiery brand of religious nationalism, termed *Africanism,* caused considerable disagreement among the CYL membership, but the worldview he articulated would resurface in new organizations. By the early fifties, League leadership had shifted to other young activists, including Oliver Tambo, Walter Sisulu, and Nelson Mandela. Their program of action put to the test the "affinity between nonviolent resistance and the ethic of Christianity," resulting in a countrywide Defiance Campaign of civil disobedience against the government.[10]

It was in the fifties that women also came prominently to the forefront of the liberation struggle. The 1952 Defiance Campaign had galvanized the masses and increased the strength of the ANC's Women's League. However, an even more pivotal development occurred the weekend of April 17, 1954, when black, white, so-called coloured (mixed ancestry), and Indian women came together to form the embryonic Federation of South African Women (FSAW). For the first time, a largely black-led movement emphasized female activism and de-emphasized male authoritarianism. Their aims were based on a women's charter with a policy that stated: "This organization is formed for the purpose of uniting all women in common action for the removal of all political, legal, economic and social disabilities."[11] The Women's Charter would be a model for the ANC's landmark Freedom Charter of 1955.

If the state regime had doubts about the independent strength and determination of women, it was to soon learn otherwise. From 1955 to 1963 hundreds of thousands of women mobilized against the government's decree that the pass laws should apply equally to African women (the laws had previously only applied to African men). On August 9, 1956, the anti-pass campaign reached a watershed moment. Answering the call of FSAW leaders Lilian Ngoyi and Helen Joseph, 20,000 women converged on Pretoria, arriving by transport and by foot, many with babies on their backs, to oppose the new law. Although the law was eventually implemented, the women-led, nonviolent campaign inspired future generations of anti-apartheid activists, especially women.[12] Today, August 9 is commemorated annually as South African Women's Day. Albertina Sisulu, past president of the FSAW and spouse of Walter Sisulu, recalls that historic day:

> I couldn't believe it when I arrived. There was a sea of women, a huge mass, oh, it was wonderful. We were so excited. We couldn't believe we were there, and so many of us. Our leaders, Lilian Ngoyi, Helen Joseph, Sophie Williams, and Rahima Moosa attempted to give our protests to the prime minister, J. G. Strijdom, but when we got there, he'd left, he'd run away.

She continues:

> When the four women returned, we stood in silent protest for thirty minutes and then started singing *Nkosi Sikeleli Afrika.* Twenty thousand women singing *Nkosi Sikeleli Afrika,* you should have heard the sound of the echoes in the Union Building. There was nothing like that sound, it filled the world. Then we sang a song of the women, *Strijdom, wathina abafazi, wathint' imbokodo, uzakufa*—Strijdom, you have tampered with the women, you have struck a rock, you have unleashed a boulder, you will die.[13]

South Africa's women, the heart and soul of the nation, had resisted state oppression with a resolve and a song that "filled the world." Undeterred by police and defense forces, their activism continued to grow in the late fifties and early sixties. The scope of their activities expanded beyond the pass laws to campaigns for domestic workers and farm laborers rights. As women filled the prisons to overflowing they were heard to sing of freedom, with fists raised high in the ANC salute. For the women's movement, much like the ANC, was rooted in an ethic and a commitment to bringing about change by peaceful means. But the horror of Sharpeville loomed on the horizon, when the pressure to reject civil disobedience and take up arms would finally erupt. So, too, would begin a new chapter of resistance song in South Africa.

War Songs of the Pan Africanist Congress

By the racist standards of the state regime, Sharpeville was a model township. A satellite of Vereeniging, a grim industrial complex fifty miles south of Johannesburg, the township had such "amenities" as running water, sanitation, streetlights, a medical clinic, and a cinema. For most of the forties and fifties neighboring whites described the township as "peaceful" and "law-abiding," and political violence was virtually unknown. Then in 1959 the seeds of political discord were sown. Unabashed government policy displaced industrial black workers for white, causing a rapid rise in black unemployment, malnutrition, and disease. Thousands of families, unable to pay the high rental costs of state-owned housing in Sharpeville, were forcibly removed to the tribal reserves.[14]

The year 1960 saw a deepening of apartheid. Spontaneous and localized actions were on the rise but, as FSAW activist and sociologist Fatima Meer noted, "Sharpeville brought to a head black agony and white tyranny."[15] On March 21, a crowd of about 5,000 answered the call of the fledgling Pan Africanist Congress (PAC) to join their Positive Action Campaign against pass laws. In a disciplined display of nonviolent civil disobedience, the demonstrators stood outside the police station and presented themselves for arrest. Suddenly, a police contingent opened fire on the group. Forty seconds and 743 bullets later, sixty-nine people lay dead; 180 more were injured. Unarmed, peaceful protesters had been fired upon by the police, and most of them were shot in the back. The combination of a poorly disciplined police force, fleeing protesters, and brutal government policies forever linked the name of Sharpeville with "massacre."

Commercial and residential panic swept South Africa's white community as strikes, protests, and demonstrations spread through other townships. On March 26, ANC president Chief Albert Luthuli publicly burned his pass and called on others to do the same. He then joined with jailed PAC president Robert Sobukwe in announcing a national day of mourning and protest on March 28, for the atrocities at Sharpeville.[16] Two days later, Nelson Mandela, Duma Nokwe, and others burned their passes in Orlando township. Young people surged into the streets singing, "Thina Silulutsha ["We are the Youth"], you will not kill us."[17] The government's response was swift, decisive, and brutal. Sobukwe was already imprisoned, and Luthuli soon followed; the PAC, ANC, and other anti-apartheid organizations were banned; and throughout the country martial law was imposed.

Forced out of the public arena, both the PAC and ANC responded by going underground and into exile to undertake military campaigns. Thus, until the emergence of the Black Consciousness Movement in the late sixties, a relative political vacuum existed in South Africa. Black Consciousness leader Stephen Biko summarized the grim situation: "So what happened was that in 1960, effectively all black resistance was killed, and the stage was left open to whites of liberal opinion to make representations for blacks, in a way that had not happened before in the past, unaccompanied by black opinion."[18]

The government's banning of opposition organizations effectively marked the end of nonviolent campaigns by the PAC. Ironically, the movement had barely made its mark before being banned. After just one year of independent existence, the two top leaders of the organization were incarcerated (Sobukwe and Potlako Leballo), and the organization had not yet built a substantial network. Still, the PAC benefited from not being an entirely new organization but "the resurgence of an historic, deep-rooted tendency in the ANC—that of African Nationalism."[19] The PAC claimed to be the true heirs of Anton Lembede, the political legatees of his belief in a mass "African" uprising to end colonialist "Boer" domination. The military wing of the PAC assumed the name Poqo—Xhosa for "standing alone" or "pure," a term first used by African independent churches in the Eastern Cape—and embarked on a program of violent action:

> We bulala
> Bulal' icolonialism
> Bulal' a mabhulu kwenzenjani
> Yiyole
> Yiyole, Yiyole le APLA
> Yiyole le APLA kwenzenjani
> [We're out to kill
> colonialism
> We're out to kill the Boers
> APLA is here
> To help us achieve our goals]

Although a few highly publicized battles against government forces occurred between 1962 and 1964 and in such places as Qamata, Rustenburg, Mbashe, Paarl, Ntlonze, Queenstown, and Mkhumbane, Poqo's general uprising did not materialize. Yet Poqo, later renamed the Azanian People's Liberation Army (APLA), did play a significant role in South African resistance in the sixties. It was the first black South African organization to embrace a strategy that explicitly called for killing people, principally whites. Moreover, as Witswatersrand University professor Tom Lodge observed, "the Poqo insurgency in certain localities attained the dimensions of a mass movement." Poqo, by the PAC's own lofty estimates, represented "the largest and most sustained African insurrectionary movement since the inception of modern African political organisations in South Africa."[20]

APLA's armed clashes with the apartheid regime were sporadic and often anemic, but they helped to keep the spirit of defiance alive in South Africa. The phoenix-like resourcefulness of the upstart PAC was clearly worrisome to new prime minister John Vorster: "We are dealing with the enemy which does not fight according to Queensbury rules. I want to say . . . if Robert Sobukwe were released we would have a fine job to do in this country."[21]

> Sizohamba No Sobukwe
> Hamba no Sobukwe
> We Sobukwe sikhokhele
> Sizongen' eAzania
> Sizongen' eAzania
> Sizongena neBazooka
> Sithi hamba we John Vorster
> Hamba we John Vorster
> We John Vorster Jimmy Kruger
> Bazohamba ngebazooka
> We'll follow Sobukwe
> We'll follow Sobukwe
> Sobukwe lead us
> We are entering Azania
> We are entering Azania
> We are entering with bazookas into Azania
> John Vorster we are warning
> you to take off (2X)
> John Vorster and Jimmy Kruger
> Will be wiped out with bazookas

The song pays tribute to the dynamism of Robert Mangaliso ("wonderful") Sobukwe, the former member of the ANC Youth League who had emerged as leader of the PAC. A tall, forceful man with a deep voice, he was known for his brilliant oratory and incisive thinking. Sobukwe had been a Methodist lay preacher, but by 1949 he had merged Christianity with the Africanism of Lembede, invoking the "God of Africa" in the cause of liberating African humanity. As PAC president, Sobukwe articulated the need for a specifically Azanian, that is to say African, destiny for the oppressed. With a flair for the polemical and the dramatic, Sobukwe's PAC gained a foothold in some regions of the country:

> Thina Isizwesintsundu
> Siyahlupheko' emhlabeni
> Siyalila kuwe Sobukwe
> Sithi zwe leth' iAfrica

Izwe lethu
Sithi izwe leth' iAfrica
Siyalila kuwe Sobukwe
Sithi zwe leth' iAfrica
[We the black nation
Are suffering here on earth
We cry out to you Sobukwe
We are crying out for our land—Africa
We are crying out for our land—Africa
We are crying for you Sobukwe
We say our land—Africa!

In PAC songs the extent of white oppression is always articulated and countered by an even more militant, at times messianic, message of black liberation. Typically, the lyrics reassert black claims that the land belongs to its rightful owners. Furthermore, freedom for Azania is prophesied to come through mass collective action by the heroes of the military resistance:

Sibane sethu maqhawe AseAzania
Ukufa kwenu akusoze kulityalwe
Ukufa kwenu kuya kukhanyi s'indlela yabo
Bonke abaphantsi kwengcinezelo
Your light you braves of Azania
Your deaths will never be forgotten
Your death will be a guiding light for the course
Of all those under oppression
Nqaphandle kwezibham nawa nothula empini
Nqaphambi kwezintlavo zezikhali
Anizanga niphelelwe yithemba laphokhona
Nathi "phambili nenkukuleko"
Even without arms you forged without a word into battle
Confronting the enemy, the enemy's rain of bullets
You never lost hope even then
You kept proclaiming: "Forward with the revolution!"
Chorus:
Siyakuzibutha izibham
Siqonde phambili ngaso sonke iskhathi
Nibe yisibane sethu maqhawe
We will pick up arms
And face forward all the time
With you braves as our guiding light

By any reasonable account, the psychological and spiritual damage caused by centuries of white domination in South Africa has been severe. Africanism was embraced as a compelling antidote to this traumatic condition, the negotiation of a new social classification that would dispel and disperse black notions of inferiority. In historical terms, the philosophy coincided with the emergence of independent African states, led by Ghana (1957) and its Pan-Africanist, anti-apartheid leader Kwame Nkrumah. The PAC's flag design underscored the movement's fervent hope in a common African destiny, a Pan-African unity: a green field with a black map of Africa marked by a gold star in the northwest, beaming light from then-revolutionary Ghana. War songs like "The Guerillas Want to Go Home to Fight" cemented the alliance between APLA forces and sympathetic frontline states. The song exhorts the allies to foment war to the fullest, by assisting APLA:

Vula Masire
Vula guerilla
Vula sigoduke
Vula Mugabe
Vula guerilla
Vula sigoduke
[Open the gates Masire (Botswana president)
Open the gates guerilla
Open and let us get home
Open the gates Mugabe (Zimbabwe president)
Open the gates guerilla
Open and let us get home]

Despite the popularity of the PAC as an alternative to the multiracialist goals of the ANC, the organization was in severe decline by the mid-sixties. Government fear of Sobukwe kept him imprisoned or under house arrest for most of the remainder of his life until he died in 1978. Inside South Africa, police arrests and infiltration shattered the movement; the external leadership, located in Dar es Salaam, was plagued by factionalism and remained in disarray for years. Only with the limited successes of Zephania Mothopeng in the seventies and his assumption of the PAC presidency in 1986, was the organization to regain a semblance of its former self.

Uphi Uphi
Nankuya nguyelo
Carebo Mothopeng
Uphi Uphi
Nguyelo nankw'esiza
Nankuya nguyelo
nguye lo nankw'esiza
Carebo Mothopeng
Mothopeng nankw'esiza
[Where is he? Where is he?
There he is, it's him

Carebo Mothopeng
Where is he, where is he?
There he is coming along
There he is, it's him
There he comes
Carebo Mothopeng
Mothopeng is coming]

In addition to reorganizing the PAC, Mothopeng, or "The Lion of Azania" as he was known, helped to establish the Young African Christian Movement in the mid-seventies. The establishment of a religious organization loosely related to the PAC dates back to the historic fusion of Christian and African elements in the movement. In the sixties Poqo formed its own church, Qamata, both a traditional and mission name for God. According to history of religions scholar David Chidester, Qamata "engaged in ritual practices, such as ceremonial initiations, war-doctoring for immunity from bullets, and invoking the ancestors, the gods of Africa, or the God of Africa, that carried the aura of a traditional African religion." A PAC activist confirms the accuracy of his analysis, recalling: "At times we would say this struggle of ours is entirely depending on the trust we have to our gods. . . . We didn't mean God; we meant the gods . . . that the ancestors are watching."[22]

But the influence of Christianity among the masses was equally palpable and had to be recognized, acknowledged, and taken seriously. The imperative, musically speaking, was to translate the power of Christian hymnody into the vernacular of the struggle. A number of PAC songs reflect this revalorization of Christian hymns, with lyrics that were revised or completely rewritten.[23] A good example of this revolutionary revisioning is "Let Us Break Chains Together with Our Guns," from the communion hymn "Let Us Break Bread Together on Our Knees." Another popular re-creation is "Lead Us Sobukwe," a political adaptation of a South African church hymn. Finally, the revised text of the African American spiritual "Plenty Good Room" sanctifies everyday acts of resistance:

We will win, there's hope enough
There's hope enough in the way we struggle
Be determined
Be determined
Brother be determined
Be determined
Sister be determined
I wouldn't be a betrayer
I'll tell you the reason why
Because I'm the people's soldier
And I will be ready to die
Chorus:
Because there's PAC, PAC, PAC

In our daily struggle
PAC, PAC
The Azanian People and God.

Weaving together religious, moral, and political sentiments in word and song, the PAC and APLA sought to prepare their followers for the apocalypse that never finally occurred. After 1978, the story of black insurgency and resistance in South Africa is largely the story of the ANC and its allies.

War Songs of the African National Congress

The time between the outlawing of South Africa's two major opposition movements and the first ANC military operation was twenty-one months. In the interim, the ANC made the strategic but reluctant transition from civil disobedience to selective use of force. In April 1961 Mandela went underground to prepare plans for military action. In December, Luthuli was awarded the Nobel Peace Prize. One week later came the change. In the early morning hours of December 16, the first of a series of some two hundred fire bombs were exploded over the next eighteen months in government buildings, post offices, and electrical substations. The historical reputation of the ANC was such that word of this first organized military response to apartheid was almost universally believed to be a Congress initiative. Umkhonto we Sizwe was launched:

> The time comes in the life of any nation when there remain only two choices: submit or fight. That time has now come to South Africa. We shall not submit and we have no choice but to hit back by all means within our power in defence of our people, our future and our freedom. . . .
>
> We of Umkhonto have always sought—as the liberation movement has sought—to achieve liberation without bloodshed and civil clash. We hope, even at this late hour, that our first actions will awaken everyone to a realization of the disastrous situation to which the Nationalist policy is leading. We hope that we will bring the government and its supporters to their senses before it is too late, so that both the government and its policies can be changed before matters reach the desperate stage of civil war.[24]

The explosive appearance of MK, accompanied by leaflets announcing its birth, had been carefully calculated to co-opt the white South African holiday known as Day of the Covenant or Dingane's Day. Dingane, the half brother of Shaka, once ruled one of the most powerful African states in southern Africa. On December 16, 1838, Boers defeated the army of the Zulu king at the battle of Blood River, so named because the nearby river ran red with Zulu blood. Politically, whites celebrated December 16 as the triumph of the Afrikaner over the African; in mythic terms, it was a perverted sacred memory that God was on their side.

The MK operation was, as journalist Howard Barrell attests, "one of the most eloquent assertions of revolutionary morality since the Second World War."[25] More so than Poqo, Umkhonto was able to offer justifications for its actions that were deeply pragmatic and rational. The ANC, so it argued, had established a long tradition of commitment to nonviolent forms of resistance and had pursued that ethic until all legal and parliamentary avenues were exhausted. Violent forms of struggle were the only means to gain a hearing, to bring the government to the negotiating table. The controlled revolutionary violence of MK, which specifically avoided attacking whites, was also a trenchant moral critique: The repressive violence of the state had bred the counterviolence of resistance.

The armed insurgency of MK was dealt a near-fatal blow in 1963. The ANC, the South African Communist Party (SACP), and the allied South Africa Congress of Trade Unions (SACTU) were devastated after police captured nearly all the leaders of the underground army, as well as valuable intelligence information, at a farmhouse in Rivonia. The evidence the police found was sufficient to convict seven of those arrested and also to levy treason charges against the commander-in-chief, Mandela.[26] The Rivonia trial, so-called, resulted in life sentences being meted out to Mandela, Sisulu and Govan Mbeki, among others. Over the next few years the police proceeded to arrest or otherwise neutralize virtually all the remaining ANC and SACP activists in the country.

In the troubled circumstances in the Congress between 1964 and 1976, Oliver Tambo gradually emerged as the de facto leader. Until 1963 he had led the ANC's external mission, establishing offices in Ghana, England, Egypt, and Tanzania. As foreign diplomatic representative, he was instrumental in forging relations with the newly organized Organization of African Unity. In the process, the ANC also became part of a loose alliance of liberation movements which derived a considerable portion of their resources from the Soviet Union and its allies. Other members were FRELIMO of Mozambique, MPLA of Angola, PAIGC of Guinea-Bissau, SWAPO of Namibia, and ZAPU of Rhodesia. After the death of Luthuli in 1967, Tambo was named acting President-General; he would lead the ANC in exile for nearly a quarter of a century.

> Uph' u Tambo
> UTamb' usehlathin' bafana
> Wenzenina?
> Uqeqesh' amajoni
> Fall in—
> one line, two lines
> [Where is Tambo?
> Tambo is in the bush, guys
> What is he doing?
> He's teaching the young fighters
> Fall in—
> One line, two lines][27]

In the late sixties the idea of black consciousness heralded the reemergence of an alternative political awareness inside South Africa. The inspiration for the movement originated in indigenous African religious movements and prophets like Anton Lembede, in attempts by Africans to regain their land, and in the trade union movement. The Congress Youth League and the PAC were also ideological forebears, but the Black Consciousness Movement had little faith in either civil disobedience or the armed struggle as the means to psychological liberation.[28] To overcome the damage wrought to the black psyche by three centuries of white supremacist rule required a different approach. Consider the theodicy of misfortune suggested by the popular song "Senzeni Na" ("What Have We Done?"):

Senzeni na senzeni na
Senzeni na senzeni na
Senzeni na senzeni na
Senzeni na kulomhlaba?
Amabhulu azizinja
Amabhulu azizinja
Amabhulu azizinja
Amabhulu azizinja
Kuyisono 'kubamnyama
Kuyisono 'kubamnyama
Kuyisono 'kubamnyama
Kuyisono kulelizwe
[What have we done, what have we done?
What have we done, what have we done?
What have we done, what have we done?
What have we done in this country (world)?
Boers are dogs
Boers are dogs
Boers are dogs
Boers are dogs
It's a sin to be black
It's a sin to be black
It's a sin to be black
It's a sin in this country (world)]

"Senzeni Na" is a deeply moving song of pain, tragedy, and lament. Its vocabulary is also that of protest, with dictions and tonalities drawn from the interior reaches of the African experience. Derived from the church, the song is often sung at funerals and rallies and written on banners and held aloft at demonstrations, marches, and meetings. The song is emblematic, says ANC stalwart Cosmo Pieterse,

of the breadth and range of the breath and soul, of the spirit, the body, the voice and feelingfulness, the timbres and evocative wholesomeness, and self-questioning, life-involving, self-empowering force that invokes all our South African time and times, people and peoples, genders, organs and generations.[29]

To its credit, "Senzeni Na" fully implicates the Boers, the agents and architects of apartheid. Still, this song, with its uneasy mix of pain and protest, lacks the crucial imperative of black re-creation according to Black Consciousness philosophy. As one South African expressed to me in private, "Blacks *know* what they have done. Blacks *know* what they have *not* done. Blacks *know* what they *must* do. There is no more time for wimpish lament, self-pity, begging or praying."

The meaning of the Black Consciousness Movement was embodied in the leadership of Bantu Stephen Biko. A charismatic proponent of black self-worth and self-determination, he rejected all white overtures in the struggle for a nonracial society. Biko confidante Barney Pityana well describes the significance of Black Consciousness: "It infused blacks with a spiritual fibre, a mettle and a fighting spirit. It is the inner soul-force seen to be invincible."[30] Dr. Mamphela Ramphele, a leader of the allied Black Women's Federation, took strong exception to gender inequities within the movement. Still, there was a sense in which Black Consciousness had liberating consequences for women:

> For the first time many black women could fall in love with their dark complexions, kinky hair, bulging hips and particular dress style. They found new pride in themselves as they were. They were no longer "non-whites," but blacks with an authentic self, appreciated on their own terms. The skin lightening creams, hot-oil combs, wigs and other trappings of the earlier period lost their grip on women.[31]

Black Consciousness spread rapidly beyond the small vanguard of university students to become a diffuse intellectual and cultural movement of artists, unionists, journalists, church people, teachers, nurses, physicians, and, especially, secondary students. For a time, the government remained surprisingly unaware of how the hegemonic foundations of apartheid itself had become the new terrain of struggle. By analyzing Eurocentric bias in institutional structures and extant relations of power—including the paternalism of white liberalism—the movement helped pave the way for an event which signaled the beginning of the end for white supremacy.

On June 16, 1976, the children of Soweto high schools assembled in protest against the government's decree that classes were to be taught in Afrikaans, the language of the oppressor. Throughout May and early June, students had demonstrated against the order without incident. The turning point was the mass meeting at Orlando West High School where police, without provocation, set the streets ablaze with tear-gas and machine-gun fire. Thirteen-year-old Hector Petersen, shot dead, was the first casualty. Then the students' fury erupted. Fighting raged and spread to other townships; edifices, personnel, and property identified with white domination were targeted. In the coming weeks and months some 700 people lost their lives in the uprisings. Over ninety percent of the dead were less than twenty-three years old. Prominent among the casualties was Steve Biko, who was beaten and tortured to death by police interrogators in September. The Soweto uprisings made international headlines, the most indicting images of South African apartheid since Sharpeville:

Emazweni
Hiyo bakhala ngathi
Bakhala ngath' emazweni
Hey bakhala ngathi
[The world over
They are crying about us
They are crying about us worldwide
Hey they are crying about us]

For the exiled ANC, the popular political upheavals paved the way for a renewal of activity inside the country. By the mid-seventies, the Congress had nearly disappeared from the articulated consciousness of antigovernment activists. Evidence indicates, however, that the Congress was able to establish underground contacts with the student insurgents and, despite pervasive police repression, offer credible assistance and cooperation. Among the youth there rose an awareness that revolution required organization and comprehensive policies capable of guiding struggle through different phases. In the end the Congress-led alliance of MK, SACP, and SACTU gained immeasurably from the new generation of radicalized recruits. As many as 4,000 women and men had left South Africa by early 1977, with about 3,000 joining the ranks of Umkhonto.[32] For the first time since the early sixties the ANC had a guerilla army, albeit small in size, that was ready to galvanize the movement into relevance. A popular song captures the extent to which many now embraced MK:

There is Sasolburg, the Supreme Court, Warmbaths,
Koeberg, Pitoli, going up in flames.
We are going there, the Umkhonto boys have arrived.
We are going there. Hayi, Hayi. We are going forward.
Don't be worried, the boys know their job.
Let Africa return.[33]

Despite the song's exclusively male imagery, women and men alike endured the hardships of warfare, voluntarily abandoning family and risking their lives for the cause. Still, the culture of combat was predominantly, and for women paradoxically, masculine in perspective. Feminist sociologist Jacklyn Cock, in her seminal study of gender and war in South Africa, notes that the image of the female fighter—the MK guerilla—became a popular mass image of the strong, liberated woman. At the same time, it was a male-defined sense of social solidarity that was validated in the subculture of armed insurgency. In the Eastern Cape province, youthful male comrades known as "Amabutho" were engaging in violent confrontation with security forces by the age of ten. Two of the most common Amabutho songs were:

The Boer is oppressing us.
The SADF [South African Defence Force]
is shooting us like animals.
Kill the Boers.

and:

We won't abandon Umkhonto we Sizwe.
These Boer blood-suckers won't get us.
We won't abandon Umkhonto we Sizwe.[34]

Events surrounding Soweto dispelled any lingering doubts about the righteousness of armed action against the forces of evil represented by the government. The townships were now in a state of open revolution. ANC president Tambo declared from headquarters in Lusaka, Zambia, that the late seventies and beyond was a time of "consolidation and further advance" that would clarify, inspire, unify, and expand the fight against injustice.[35]

The problem facing the military wing of the ANC was how to turn thousands of raw recruits not just into guerilla fighters but into politically responsible cadres. In the hazardous conditions of camps in Zambia, Tanzania, Mozambique (briefly), and especially Angola, what became known as the "June 16 Detachment" met the *umgwenya*, veterans of earlier campaigns. Military deployment with other liberation armies, most notably the Zimbabwe African People's Union (ZAPU) and the South West African People's Organization (SWAPO), was a true "baptism of fire." For others, advanced training in select countries, including the Soviet Union, East Germany, and Cuba proved key.

Amaqwala alshetshele morawo
Uyarona bapelo bothatha kopelo
Uyarona
Uyarona
Uyarona bopelo botha kopelo
Cowards are sneaking to the back
We are going forth irrespective of the risk to our lives
We are going
We are going
We are going despite the risk to our lives
Chorus:
Siyaya siyaya siyayabo
Siyaya sobona masotsha omkhonto
Siyaya siyaya siyayabo
Siyaya sobona masotsha e SWAPO
Oh we are going, we are going, yes we are going
We are going to see Mkhonto soldiers

We are going, we are going, yes we are going
We are going to see SWAPO soldiers
Mkhonto soldiers
SWAPO soldiers

Throughout the eighties, the primary mission of Umkhonto was to link its own underground activity to local above-ground campaigns. To be seen and heard, to be recognized, acknowledged, and taken seriously by the government, MK activity had to escalate mass action and further popularize the ANC. The shifting emphasis toward what was called the "people's army" and "people's war" effected a new self-understanding within the ANC. The transformation of Umkhonto into a populist army signified a type of spiritual politics that inspired the nonwhite community, and not a few whites, to greater acts of resistance and sacrifice.

Joyna joyna joyna mntwanam
Sikhon 'isbham sokulshaya amabhulu
Macommisa
Siwelele ma
Yoizo joyna mnlanam
Join join join my child
The guns are here/available for hitting the boers
Commissars
Let us cross into our country
Come and join [the ANC] my child

Singing remained essential to building movement momentum throughout the eighties. Through song, women and men, boys and girls, took part in subversive discourse, in a politicized way of questioning and knowing, about their social circumstance. Liberation song was unifying and attested to the limits of state power versus the power of "the people." In point of fact, no amount of government resolve could quell the insurrectionary power of song. However, state authorities could prohibit the airplay, sale, and possession of "treasonous" recordings. According to social critic Ian Kerkhof, the penalty for transgression of such laws was severe:

Arrests and convictions in terms of censorship legislation occur with distressing regularity: Jacob Mashigo received five years imprisonment in August 1983 for possessing a cassette with *one song* by Miriam Makeba and Harry Belafonte. Thabo Moloi received two years imprisonment for possessing a cassette with a speech by ANC President Oliver Tambo, interspersed with Freedom songs. Derek Tsietsi Makomoreng received five years imprisonment in January this year for possessing a 60 minute cassette with the music of the ANC Cultural Ensemble Amandla on it.[36]

For its part, the Congress's exile headquarters encouraged and mobilized its constituents from abroad. Radio Freedom beamed ANC news and information into South Africa daily from broadcasting facilities in Zambia, Ethiopia, Angola, Madagascar, and Tanzania. One of the most highly valued of the stations' services was, of course, song. For it was song, along with news and information, that best helped to convey the objectives of the struggle. Hence, the "Chant by the Militants" exhorted its listeners to prepare for the new political dispensation:

Company
Tshela wena, tshelu uTambo
Siyal'thatha, kulonyaka
Tambo ye, yicomanda
NoMandela, basemajele
NoSisulu, basemajele
Sibakhulule
Lenj'u Botha
Usengozini
No Kruger
Usengozini
No LeGrange
Usengozini
Shoot to kill! Guerilla!
[Company
Tell, tell, Tambo
We'll take our country this year
Tambo is our commander
And Mandela, in jail
And Sisulu, in jail
We will release them
That dog Botha
Is in danger
And Kruger
Is in danger
And LeGrange
Is in danger
Shoot to Kill! Guerilla!

So, too, did the song "Mandela," with its strong messianic undertones:

Hebathi uyeza
Hebathi uyeza uMandela
Sowashaya amabhunu
[We hear he is coming
We hear that Mandela is coming
We will beat the racist whites][37]

By contesting the regime's alleged control of the airwaves, the ANC-led alliance was able to communicate a powerful alternative message to the rank and file. The government had tried to control all forms of media, but the resistance movement was successful in unleashing its own interpretation of events. As the eighties progressed, South Africa was convulsed with deepening conflict, portending revolutionary change. In the decade that the ANC called the "Decade of Liberation," the study of war was being painfully transformed into a preparation for democracy.

Freedom's Song

On February 11, 1990, Nelson Mandela walked out of Victor Verster prison near Cape Town. With the entire world looking on, he emerged after twenty-seven years of confinement unbowed and unbroken, an August picture of quiet dignity and strength. Later that day, addressing an estimated crowd of 100,000, Mandela said, "I stand before you not as a prophet, but as a humble servant of you, the people. Your tireless and heroic sacrifices have made it possible for me to be here today. I therefore place the remaining years of my life in your hands."[38] Not a prophet, Mandela nevertheless came out of prison as a promise of the future, a living symbol of resistance, hope, and change.[39]

In the person and presence of "Madiba"—Mandela's clan name and a title of deep respect—a new stage in the struggle for a democratic, nonracial, and nonsexist South Africa found life. Mandela's release, coupled with the unbanning of the ANC, SACP, PAC, and other African political organizations, deepened and accelerated the struggle to dismantle apartheid. The insurgent mass mobilization in the weeks and months following Mandela's release, up to the holding of the first one-person, one-vote elections in the history of the country, was the culmination of a long and epic struggle.

In the nineties the mass democratic movement linked with the ANC remained committed to the racial inclusiveness that had characterized it for decades, but its views had matured beyond the earlier loose political alliances characterized by "multiracialism" to a more democratic and unitary "nonracialism" in which anti-apartheid opponents, regardless of classification ("Indians," "Coloured," "White," "Asians," "Blacks") or ideology (communist, socialist, traditionalist), were fully accepted within the ranks. Even many black consciousness proponents came to support the larger scope for humanity now represented by the ANC. It proved to be a far more difficult step for the ANC to next implement a "nonsexism" blueprint for the nation. Take this song, which praises women while reinforcing traditional gender role expectations:

Khaya bakulindile
Malibongwe igama lamakosikazi
Akukho ntomb' esakimfazwe
[They are waiting for you at home
Praise be to women
No woman is afraid of the revolution

Movement activist Sethembile N. rightly voiced disappointment with ANC policy, saying that "the struggle is retarded when fifty percent of the population is not fully involved in it. How will the movement even *get* liberation if women are waiting *until* liberation to be involved?"[40]

The role of sexism in the lives of South African women has long been obscured by a myriad of historical and social factors. For generations, repressive state policies—from the Group Areas Act to influx control, coupled with the migrant labor system—have destroyed African family life. In addition, white middle-class women's groups have typically expressed women's solidarity in a way that belied their gross insensitivity to the struggles of black working-class women. As Cock so adroitly notes, these and other factors led many African women to view feminism as a bourgeois interest and the family "as an arena to be defended against the encroachments of the apartheid state."[41]

Apartheid and sexism are, in complex respects, so intertwined that fighting one ought to necessarily entail fighting the other. In other instances, the horrors of patriarchy—domestic servitude, violence, sexual harassment, rape, and assault—can and must be distinguished from racism. Thus while many women may be critical of "feminism," nearly all are committed to "women's rights." The ANC's Women's League, in particular, has taken the active lead in addressing sexism and gender inequality.[42]

The Congress overall has been slower to embrace the emancipation of women as more than a by-product of the democratic movement. In a November 1990 speech entitled "The Women's Movement Must Play a Central Role," Mandela challenged the ANC leadership to end gender discrimination within its ranks as well as in society at large.[43] Still, the absence of women at decision-making levels remained glaringly apparent. Today, the Mandela-led government includes some, though disproportionately few, women. In truth, no contradiction exists between national liberation and women's liberation—except to the extent that men make it so:

Ndizwa Ingoma [I hear singing]
Ndizwa iskhalo [I hear crying]
Listen to the cries
of women as if they
are humming a song
Ndizwa Ingoma
Ayangqikaza ayesaba
Amaqwala:
"Cowards are dithering
Cowards are scared
Cowards say let's go back"
Freedom is their birthright
But gross and brutal exploitation
is their experience[44]

With the power of an African drum, Mzwakhe Mbuli's bass voice sounds forth. Mbuli, known as the "people's poet," has stirred stadiums of people to consciousness and action for more than a decade. His songs are noted for their richness in evocative imagery, emitting from his intense involvement in the struggle. The song "Ndizwa Ingoma" ("I Hear Singing") is an anomaly—a progressive male response to the oppression of women. In addition, it pays homage to "Ayangqikaza Ayesaba Amaqwala," a women's song of liberation. The rap group 200 IQ presents an even more energetic critique of sexism in "Democracy (Voice of a Woman)":

> Some male people, they bold and arrogant, vain,
> and using us women to compete with . . .
> But now there are those who want to race
> but don't consider losing face.
> It's penalties for those who don't do right
> and just depressing everyone—women taking a lot of stressing!
> It's not her fault that your thoughts are shrinking while hers are
>   growing . . .
> Know too, we gotta have a leader of our own likeness.
> So release all your shyness and call me your highness, away with the
>   tale of the weaker sex.[45]

The certitude that the future belonged to the nonracial and increasingly nonsexist democratic movement led by the ANC was not shared by everyone. To begin with, the ANC had to stake its claims on the future in negotiations with the National Party government. But other movements also challenged any exclusive, privileged claims to power on the part of the African National Congress. The Azanian People's Organization (AZAPO), a black consciousness group, and the Pan Africanist Congress of Azania (PAC) both enjoyed a modicum of public support. AZAPO rejected the proposed talks with the government, insisting that "negotiations should take place among resistance organizations of the black people, not with the ruling class."[46] The PAC was similarly opposed to any settlement with the "illegal" racist regime. Hence this song, the repetitive nature of which leaves no one in doubt as to the PAC's contemptuous view of the negotiations:

> Soke sbone thina amanegotiations
> We are watching the so-called negotiations
> Soke sbone thina amanegotiations
> We are watching [with curiosity] the negotiations
> Soke sbone thina amanegotiations
> We are watching [with curiosity] the negotiations

While the political momentum was with negotiation and national reconciliation, violence continued to sweep the country. At the center of the violence was Chief Mangosuthu Gatsha Buthulezi and the Inkatha Freedom Party. During the second half of the eighties, Buthelezi's homeland of KwaZulu and the surrounding region of Natal became one of the most violent places on earth. By late 1990 the epicenter of violence had shifted to the townships around Johannesburg. The body count was well into the thousands by early 1994, as South Africa was engulfed in an apparently interminable state of war between Inkatha forces and supporters of ANC-affiliated organizations. From the standpoint of other African groups, who were occasionally involved in violent confrontations with each other, the steady escalation in violence was cause for deep concern, evidence these songs:

> Ngaba Yini Sekunjenjenje na
> Luphelil'uthando kwanesimilo
> Abantu bayabulalana
> Abadala kwanabancinane
> Bawo baxolele
> Buyisa iingqondo zethu
> Ziphuthume ukulunga
> Mas 'bambaneni, mas 'bambaneni
> Mas 'bambaneni, Ma Africa
> Phantsi ngodlano
> Phezulu ngoxolo
> [How did it get to this?
> Love and respect is gone
> People are killing each other
> The old and the young
> God please forgive them
> Restore our sanity
> Enable us to recover our goodness
> Let's unite, let's unite
> Let's unite, fellow Africans
> Down with interfighting
> Up with peace

Of course, scholars and journalists amply documented how "right-wing forces within the police and military intelligence either actively foment black violence and exploit cleavages or do not care much to suppress black violence."[47] In addition to covert involvement in ethnic conflict in the early nineties, state security forces were directly implicated in the deaths of many hundreds more. In the face of strategic state repression, the recalcitrance of Inkatha and anti-apartheid factionalism, the ANC nonetheless retained the political initiative.

By 1993 a broadening alliance of democratic forces that included the Congress of South African Trade Unions, several Bantustan governments, the SACP, and other organizations had joined with the ANC in advancing a series of demands: the return of exiles, the release of political prisoners, the repeal of discriminatory laws, the establishment of an interim government, and a democratically elected constituent assembly to draft a new constitution. Out of this forceful détente, April 26–28, 1994, were the dates set for the first nonracial elections in South African history. The ANC, a banned organization barely four years earlier, launched an election campaign with the goal of winning a decisive majority.

We mama no baba [Mother and father]
Wwe sisi no bhuti [Sister and brother]
Inkululeko ifikile [Freedom is here]
Ashambeni sovota [let's go vote]
Vote ANC, ANC, ANC . . .
Sekunjalo [Now is the time]
Kinakayo [Now is the time]
People let's vote
ANC, ANC, ANC . . .

The longest popular struggle for democracy on the African continent ended in 1994 with the transfer of power to black majority rule, and the assumption by Mandela and the African National Congress of state governance. The ANC victory song "Ha A Yo" ("There Is No One [Quite Like Them]"), opens with the famous last words spoken by Mandela to the court before being sentenced to life imprisonment in June 1964. He used these same words in celebrating his release, citing their continued relevance:

I have fought against white domination, and I have fought against black domination. I have cherished the ideal of a democratic and free society in which all persons live together in harmony and with equal opportunities. It is an ideal which I hope to live for, and to see realized. . . . If needs be, it is an ideal for which I am prepared to die.

Mandela's words were later affixed to music. On Sunday afternoon, April 10, 1994, at Soweto's Orlando East stadium, tens of thousands of South Africans hailed the arrival of the President-in-waiting, to loud and festive song:

Nelson Mandela, Nelson Mandela
Hayo otswana leyena [There is no one quite like him]
Like Xuma and Luthuli before them
With people of the world around them
They took on the might of the government
To bring all the changes we see
They landed in prison and exile
Determined, courageous, and steadfast
They took on the might of the government
To bring all the changes we see
Nelson Mandela
Oliver Tambo
Hayo otswana leyena . . . Walter Sisulu
Govan Mbeki

Albert Luthuli
Nelson Mandela
Wilton Mkwayi
Hayo otswana leyena . . . Raymond Mhlaba
Ahmed Kathrada
Suhe Rifala
Andrew Mlangeni
Now is the time to vote for peace,
justice, freedom, and democracy.
Mayibuye, iAfrica! [Come back, Africa!]
Nelson Mandela, Nelson Mandela
Hayo otswana leyena [There is no one quite like him][48]

The song and occasion provided an opportunity for supporters of the ANC to remember their fallen heroes (but no "sheroes") with gratitude, and to look with confidence to the new inclusive South Africa. The nation had reached a watershed between a brutal past and a future which provided untold opportunities for "peace, justice, freedom, and democracy" for black and white together.

The process now underway in South Africa is that of developing the detailed policy and legislative program necessary to meet the vast needs of the people. Ultimately, the task of reconstruction, development, and reconciliation will prove far more demanding, challenging, and rewarding than the struggles of the past. Much remains to be done to establish some semblance of social and economic parity and a lasting political peace. The challenge for music, now as before, is to redefine resistance with fresh insight and energy. To sing songs that express ever more eloquently the struggles of the distraught and unheralded— the unskilled laborer, the dispossessed widow, the battered woman, the malnourished child, the victim of AIDS. To give voice to aspirations that are nonpartisan, nonviolent, and, most of all, redemptive. Still, the initial political objective has been accomplished. The people of South Africa resisted injustice, perversion, and evil—and won.

THE RHYTHM OF EVERYDAY POLITICS | Public Performance and Political Transitions in Mali

ZERIC KAY SMITH

"Lib-er-é! Mar-I-ko! Lib-er-é! Mar-I-ko!" "Liberate Mariko" was the rally cry of young students throughout the West African nation of Mali in 1991. The leader of the Association of Malian Students and Pupils (AEEM), Oumar Mariko, had been imprisoned by the military regime of President Moussa Traoré for persistent attempts to organize an independent student union with no ties to the government. The students went on a nationwide strike to press for his release and for other demands. As part of the strike, marches were organized in many cites and towns. The pattern of mobilization that the AEEM followed was for the older students (grades seven through twelve) to leave their schools and circulate to the elementary schools calling for their young comrades to join them. They would then march through the streets chanting, sometimes singing, in protest of the regime. During one such protest, I was surprised to hear a group of young students who marched past the market in the town of Bougouni chanting "Li-ber-té! Marl-bor-o!" rather than the expected "Lib-er-é! Mar-I-ko!" *Liberté* is the name of a common brand of cigarette sold in Mali while Marlboro is, of course, the famous American cigarette brand name that is also widely available there. Instead of the message of political liberation, these younger students were mistakenly chanting the names of the tobacco products that they often are sent to buy on the errand of their older siblings, cousins, or neighbors. Though they got the detail of the names wrong, their rhythmic sense was right on track. Certainly in this case, the rhythm was more important than the lyric.

Living and working in Mali for over two years, my wife and I witnessed and participated in a large number of important social events. During prosaic gatherings of friends, naming ceremonies for new babies, weddings, religious and state holidays, and even during two months of civil unrest now known in Mali as "the peoples revolution" in which the military dictator of twenty-eight years was brought down by popular protest, rhythmic accompaniment was ever present. This paper will explore the rhythmic qualities of everyday politics in Mali and will provide examples of how a macro-rhythm or pattern of social and political expectations has had significant impact on the ongoing political transition in this African nation. I will look at two levels of rhythm: actual percussion will be referred to as micro-rhythms, while macro-rhythms will indicate long-term patterns or expectations of governance in Mali.[1] The micro and the macro are interpenetrated and constantly re-create each other, but an attempt to conceptually separate them should allow a better understanding of how they work together.[2] To make this distinction I will first give examples of the most common types of rhythm, then I will provide a short exploration of the clear connection between public performance and rhythm. Finally I will show how public performance can sometimes serve to link micro- and macro- rhythms. This happens when political themes enter into public performance and when public performance itself becomes a political act. At these moments, rhythm itself serves political ends. It is the contention of this article that the boundary between political action and performance is sometimes nonexistent and that it is rhythm that serves to link the two in contemporary Malian politics.

Rhythm in Everyday Life—*Le cadence du travail*

The micro-rhythms of daily life in Mali are present in a wide variety of activities and events. Rhythm is not only central in music, which is at the heart of almost all social gatherings, it also plays an important role in work activities. Most women in Mali have the task of pounding millet, corn, or rice for daily meals. This is done with the use of a large wooden mortar into which the grain is placed, and a heavy pestle that is lifted and then thrown down onto the grain. Pounding grain takes from fifteen minutes to an hour depending on the amount and type of grain and the dish that is being prepared. Often two or more women will pound grain with multiple pestles in the same mortar and the rhythm of the pounding will be enhanced by clapping and feet stamping timed so that the pestle never misses a beat. I often astounded families in villages that I visited for the first time after I learned to pound millet. Not only did they enjoy the novelty of a white man doing "women's" work, but when I did a double clap between beats, the woman with whom I pounded with would always laugh heartily.

Agricultural work also has an important rhythmic dimension. Using short-handled hoes called *dabas* and machetes, Malian men and women cultivate large fields of grain, peanuts, vegetable gardens, etc. Large work groups usually have a percussionist in the field, and smaller groups make their rhythm with their tools. Mounding hills, weeding, and harvesting are all done with these tools, and the strokes of the daba must match those you work beside or gentle teasing is sure to follow. I was once the target of such joking when some friends and I were out chopping posts for a garden fence. I was using the machete to chop a small tree and I was not making very quick progress. I was in a crowded thicket and couldn't get a full swing at the notch that I had cut, nor could I see well because of the sweat in my eyes. As I struggled to hit the wood harder my friends laughed and told me *"Ce n'est pas la force, c'est la cadence du travail"* ("It's not strength, but the rhythm of the work").

The blacksmith's forge provides another example of micro-rhythms in Mali. As described by McNaughton:

> Pushing air through . . . bellows produces a wonderful sonorous blast, which can be heard all around the forge and the immediate vicinity. The skins are pushed alternately, at first in a very even two beat rhythm. . . . Gradually the apprentice learns to gauge how much vigor to apply to his work, and in the process he begins to vary his basic two-beat rhythm. The result is patterns of rhythm that resemble drum beats, except that the percussive thrust of drumming is replaced by fluid gusts of air.[3]

Each smith adds his own distinct percussive pattern to the steady beat he learned as an apprentice, and these rhythms can become quite complex. McNaughton also observed women who pounded millet near the smith's forge, and while they worked the smith played the bellows in counterpoint to the mortar and pestles.[4] Thus "the most mundane, tedious task imaginable . . . becomes something quite wonderful and anything but boring. It acquires pleasing articulation, according to the dictates of traditional music aesthetics."[5]

The Rhythm of Politics in Public Performance

Whether by a griot, a theater troupe, professional musicians, or whole communities, public performances are quite common in Mali. They occur to mark marriages, births and deaths, the start and end of the agricultural season, civil and religious holidays, and for many other reasons. The link between public performance and micro-rhythm is obvious, and there has been much written on the various types of public performance in Mali and neighboring countries.[6]

Speaking of women's dances in urban Senegal, Heath writes, "As performance genres, they are marked forms generally reserved for extraordinary occasions, in contrast to the unmarked, ongoing activities of daily life."[7] Though public performances are marked and set apart, they draw on the same musical aesthetics as the daily examples of rhythm provided above. They also serve many of the same purposes. Heath finds certain women's dances to be a site of resistance to male domination and an arena in which various forms of political and social domination are reinforced.[8] Public performances also provide an arena for political conflict in which issues of both local and national interests are debated.[9] While performance often serves to reinforce the hegemonic interpretation of issues by the powerful, at key moments a discourse of dissent can also emerge.[10] The example of a puppet masquerade theater in central Mali provides an illustration of how this discourse can sometimes be manifest.

For at least the past century, in the quarter of Kirango near the Markala Dam in central Mali, the young men's club, (ages from twenty to forty), has organized an annual puppet theater, mask festival, and village dance. The masks that are danced in this festival represent a wide variety of animals, people, and mythical characters that are important in the cultural and social life of this town. Though the explicitly religious nature of the festival was abandoned in the thirties when most of the towns families became Muslim, the festival itself has grown in size. The puppets and masks have also grown, becoming more elaborate as they wear out and are replaced by new figures.

Since 1991, when Mali's military ruler of two decades was replaced by first a transitional and then an elected government, street marches and demonstrations have been common. As described at the start of this paper, students and young people in the major cities of the country used these tactics repeatedly to press for their political demands which served as the spark for Traoré's downfall and have proven very difficult for the newly elected regime as well. This pattern repeats itself in the case of Kirango.

Ba Boré is forty years old, but when his father died fifteen years ago, Boré was considered too young to assume his role as the hereditary chief of the village. By mutual agreement with the village council, Coulibaly took on the role of chief with the understanding that when Ba Boré came of age he would be made chief.

This arrangement seemed to work fine for a decade, but in the past few years increasing conflict has developed between Coulibaly and the village council. Early in 1993, Coulibaly went to the Chief d'Arrondissement (the lowest level national government representative) and requested that he be made the official village chief. He argued that the "traditional" chief was illiterate in French and could not get anything done. Coulibaly on the other hand had been serving as chief for fifteen years and felt his position should be formalized and made official. Without consulting the village council, the Chief d'Arrondissement agreed and made Coulibaly chief. The village council was livid and from that point on they refused to go to meetings when Coulibaly called them. Instead, if Coulibaly sent messages to them about a meeting they would show up at the home of Ba Boré and say, "We heard the chief called a meeting, here we are."

Boré was a reluctant participant in this conflict until the village dance festival was threatened. Boré was the leader of the young men's organization that was responsible for the festival. Each year, to pay for new costumes, masks, and other items associated with the festival, each family in the quarter is assessed a payment. This usually consists of a bag of rice and some variable amount of money. Coulibaly refused to pay the money or the rice though he is one of the more wealthy people in the quarter. In response, the organizers told him he would not be invited to attend the festival. This absence would be tantamount to admitting he had no support from the people of the quarter, and so a few days later he announced that because of the increasing wasteful costs associated with the festival and because it contradicted Islam, the festival would be canceled.

In the following days meetings were held and supporters of Boré organized what they called a "Democracy March." The week before the festival was supposed to take place hundreds of people marched three miles through town to the office of the Chief d'Arrondissement located in nearby Markala. They demanded that their festival be restored and that Boré be made the official chief of Kirango. The Chief d'Arrondissement said that they could have the festival but did not make a decision about the chief.

With the festival restored, Coulibaly let it be known that he was planning on taking his rightful place as chief at the festival. Because of his attempt to cancel the festival, however, most of those who had previously supported him turned against him, and he stayed away for all three days of the festival. The attendance at the festival was lower than it had been in the past few years. Some told me that this was because the supporters of Coulibaly stayed away, while others said it was because many in outlying villages received the message that the festival was canceled and did not find out that it was reinstated. In any case the festival took place and the chair of the chief was vacant except for a few times when some friends of Boré forced him to sit in it, seemingly as a sign of defiance.

The Kirango festival itself not only shows how political questions and performance can be intermingled, but the evolution of the masquerade over time also reflects a social and political rhythm. The residents of Kirango repeated what had become a familiar national beat when they expressed their grievances in the form of the democracy march. Like the students in the regional and national capitols, they drew on the rhetorical legitimacy lent to them by the term *democracy*. In this march and in the festival that resulted from it, micro- and macro-rhythms united to correct a social and political situation that a large percentage of Kirango's residents felt was offbeat. Coulibaly was not perceived as an illegitimate leader simply because he was not born the son of a chief. The fact that he functioned as chief for years and the lack of a strict lineage based succession pattern among the Bamana indicate that this is not the case. Instead Coulibaly became unacceptable when he overstepped his authority and attempted to cancel the festival in order to preserve his political position. This illegitimate use of power serves as an important link as I now explore the patterns and expectations of power which I have called macro-rhythms.

Macro-Rhythms, Political Theater, and the Theater of Politics

In Mali, national politics seems to sound a regular beat and to provide an articulation familiar to Malians.[11] The Kirango masquerade, like similar celebrations in the surrounding region of Segou, has evolved from depictions of hunting and fishing into a form that tends to stress the importance of community life.[12] With such figures as the "colonial officer on horseback," "President Traoré," and a patriotic bird called the "Malikono,"[13] the form of the masquerade also picks up political themes of national importance. The macro-rhythms of national politics are played out and reflected in communities all over Mali. These macro-rhythms are the common patterns and expectations of politics. They include certain expectations about the exercise of legitimate power and assumptions about the duties of citizens vis-à-vis, *le pouvoir,* "power."[14] These expectations and assumptions can be summarized by a list of key concepts, including reciprocity of power, local autonomy, trust and cooperation across various social cleavages, and tolerance of diversity.[15] The importance of these concepts can be detected in a wide variety of contemporary and historical settings. As they appear, are employed and modified, and then reappear in different contexts, they begin to form the pattern of expectations that typifies Malian political culture. These patterns are rhythmic not only because of their consistency, but also because, like a polyrhythmic drum beat from a Malian musical ensemble, they are multilayered and never completely static. Below I provide a sampling from my own experiences to illustrate how historical understandings and expectations sometimes dictate and often influence contemporary Malian politics. The consistent repetition of these themes across time and geographic space brings a rhythm to Malian political experience and is at the heart of Mali's culture of politics.[16]

I recently interviewed the chief of Kangaba. Kangaba, a village in southern Mali, is often called by its traditional name, Kaba. Kaba was the center of the Empire of Mali and home of the legendary figure Sundiata Keita during the fourteenth century. The village chief, Sori Keita, is the traditionally recognized heir to the power of Sundiata. He is a living symbol of the ancient Malian empire from which the modern nation took its name. Within the village of Kaba is a sacred hut that is believed to be constructed on the spot where Sundiata lived. A village organization provides for the upkeep of the hut, and sacred rites are occasionally held inside it; otherwise it is sealed tightly.

Sori Keita has been chief of Kaba since the mid-sixties, and as such he has personally hosted every president of Mali. Each president has made a pilgrimage of sorts to this small town on the frontier with Guinea. Keita, along with some of the village elders, share a common interpretation of the meaning of these visits. "They come to give honor to the empire which gave our nation its name." In some cases they also come for personal political gain and increased national legitimacy. Modibo Keita, the first president of Mali, went there in 1968. This was not his first visit to Kaba, but at this time he told the Chief that he wanted to go inside the sacred hut. He was told that he could not as he was not an initiate of the society that keeps the secrets of the hut. He became angry and said rude things to the people of Kangaba and then left. "Less than two months later," the chief said, "Modibo had fallen." President Modibo Keita indeed fell in a coup in October 1968. The military officer who replaced Keita, Moussa Traoré, was the next president to visit Kaba.

Village chief Keita related how Traoré honored and respected the people of Kaba on many visits over the years he was in power. His final visit in the fall of 1990 was different however. On this visit he took the people of Kaba to task for not working hard enough in their fields and for spending too much time digging for treasure in the nearby gold mines. Keita and the village elders told me that Traoré too was deposed soon after he turned his back on Kaba.

Even the interim head of state, Amadou Toumani Toure, who was the leader of the coup that deposed Traoré and served as president of the republic for less than a year, made a visit to Kaba. His visit was uneventful though Keita commented that Toure had paid appropriate respect and would have success in the future because of it.

Keita said that he was very impressed with the new president, Konaré, because, "not only did he visit but he sat here on the ground for two or three hours and listened to us and our problems. He did not tell us what to do, he listened." That was a sign of a good leader in his mind. He said that Sundiata was not a dictator but that he defeated Sumangoro who was. I have heard this a number of times, and it seems to be a widely held contemporary interpretation of the Sundiata epic that Sundiata came to defeat dictatorship and to restore freedom to Mali.

This was certainly the belief of Boubacar Traoré, an electrician that I met on public transport one day in Bamako. With only the knowledge that I was interested in Malian politics, he immediately began to talk about the importance of knowing Malian history and culture to understand Malian politics. He said: "Pour governer Mali, il faut avoir bonne conseil" ["To govern Mali, you must have good advice"]. Malians expect their leaders to listen to them. They must respect the ideas of equality, tolerance and humanism along with freedom."[17] He repeatedly used the example of Sumangoro and Sundiata as models of bad and good rulers. Sundiata Keita, the founder of the kingdom of Mali, is widely celebrated in oral epics recited by griots in much of modern Mali.[18] In the epic, Sundiata defeated the impostor king Sumangoro to take his rightful place as leader. The electrician used these figures as symbols to refer to modern political events.

> Sumangoro forced people to work while Sundiata gave freedom to people but he still demanded work, but not work for the king, work for personal benefit. Democracy means freedom in Mali, but freedom from what? We haven't yet told the people that freedom from certain unpopular taxes does not mean freedom from hard work. Some people think that democracy means freedom to take what you want. This was not so with Sundiata, he made Mali free but also demanded people to work for themselves. With Sumangoro you would work a field and at harvest time the tax collector would come and take it all and you would have to go and get only enough to feed your family week by week. Sundiata let you keep all you grew and only demanded a small percentage for his army to protect you. Sundiata freed everyone, he decentralized everything and gave people liberty to speak, and freedom to work for themselves. We must be careful though because too much liberty without discipline can lead to laziness and banditry.
>
> We don't need millions of dollars, we need to have work, we need equality, tolerance and humanism and we get examples of these qualities from our own experience. Mali is a very old nation. Everything has a base, to build a house, build the basement well. *Yani I ka jigi I bin yoro la, I bé jigi I talo yoro la.* If you fall, instead of looking at the place you landed, demand the few steps before.[19]

It is striking that in the cases of Kaba's chief Sori Keita and the electrician Traoré both, we see a common interpretation of the character and meaning of Sundiata. This points up a number of the macro-rhythms that I have referred to such as tolerance, reciprocal power, and local autonomy or freedom. In addition, the pattern of repeated presidential visits to a small village is also another level of rhythm that connects the everyday activities of Malians to their religious and cultural celebrations and to national political expectations. These links between religion, culture, and politics are not new in Mali. Mali's first president, Modibo Keita, made extensive use of cultural symbols throughout his tenure.

> President Modibo Keita, man of faith, always worked hard to spread many ideals. All of Africa was his battle field. His ultimate objective was to give back to Africa its dignity which had long been flouted. He wanted to erase the humiliations caused to our continent. He wanted a new Africa, reconciled with itself and master of its own destiny. A man of sacrifice, fundamentally fair, sweet with a profound humility, state power was not his goal. He did not cling to it. What pre-occupied him before all else, was the message he gave to his people and to all of Africa: Justice, Liberty, Dignity and Independence.[20]

These opening lines to a book on the political accomplishments of Mali's first president sound almost like the opening lines in a praise poem or epic. Hopkins describes the Keita regime's politics as being "based on traditional Malian values reinforced at key points by Leninist theory."[21] Hopkins points out that by 1965, pragmatic politics had replaced ideological politics in Malian political life.[22] The ideological politics that he speaks of are both rooted in, and in conflict with, well-established expectations of governance in Mali. I maintain that an important part of the reason that Keita eventually lost popular support was because he moved away from the ideals and expectations of Mali's culture of politics—its macro-rhythms.

Throughout his public life, Keita used imagery and symbols that drew on the historic glory of Mali and specifically on the importance of Sundiata. Keita received education in the colonial system and ultimately attended the elite Ecole de William-Ponty in Senegal. Returning to the French Sudan (the colonial name of Mali) with a teaching degree, he quickly became involved in some of the many voluntary organizations that sprung up in Bamako during the thirties.

A group that Keita helped to organize, Art et Travail, wrote and acted historical plays based on the lives of Malian heroes. The exploits and heroic acts of Sundiata and other Malian heroes were portrayed by this theater group during the pre-independence period. These productions, though allowed for a time by the colonial administration, were recognized to contain political protest, and it ultimately became clear that the cultural objectives of these groups also served anti-colonial goals.[23] Many of these groups resisted or refused French attempts to alter the text of plays that French authorities feared would encourage political resistance.[24]

The theater continued to carry political importance into the post-independence era. Hopkins describes a play performed by a youth group in a drama competition which satirizes a French attempt to provoke a coup in Mali. This was used to show support of the Keita regime's monetary reforms.

Modern theater was not the only type of popular culture to contain political messages during this time period. Meillassoux describes the *koteba* as the popular comic street theater of Bamako.[25] The *koteba* has its origins in rural villages and was brought to the capital where it is now often performed on the street in front of a family compound for special social occasions such as marriages. The *koteba* usually offers a series of stereotyped characters; it serves primarily to criticize the inconsistent behavior of others but does not question the legitimacy of the social structure itself. Those who are often criticized and made fun of include the lazy peasant, the hypocritical *marabout* (Muslim holy man) or perhaps members of neighboring ethnic groups.

Meillassoux sees the modern theater groups such as Art et Travail as having more relevant critiques of social structure and says that the koteba is "but the reflection of a society which is in the course of disappearing in the new town structures."[26] He provides evidence, however, of considerable political content in "koteba." Besides the ability of young people to criticize respected leaders, there are other important political implications in *koteba*. Meillassoux describes a play in which villagers are summoned to pay a tax by an African representative of the colonial administration. The tax collector allows himself to be bribed and he then tries to confuse the issue with the local French captain. "The captain goes to the village and each villager tells him a different version of the way the tax was collected so that he gets muddled up and leaves the village in a great fluster."[27] Meillassoux recognizes that this play points out the corruption and ineptitude of the French and that it also shows collective resistance to colonial constraints; but he maintains that, in the main, *koteba* is not a particularly progressive force and is concerned with maintenance of the social status quo rather than revolutionary change. I would argue that in the context of pre-independence Sudan, this particular episode of *koteba* shows a remarkable awareness of the collective power of villagers to deal with a perceived injustice. Certainly as a model and inspiration for much modern theater, the ability of *koteba* to act as a voice for social criticism is worth noting. It is within this context that Keita and his associates used the power of modern theater in their quest for independence. After gaining independence and winning elections that brought them to power in 1960, Keita and his party, the US-RDA, continued to follow the macro-rhythms of Malian politics.

Throughout his political career, Modibo Keita made consistent reference to traditional values and often appealed to the historical legacy of the empire of Mali. Often these references were attempts to link his regime to the glory of the past and thus to legitimize current policies. Keita wanted to develop a certain set of national values and virtues that would assure Mali of development, unity, and tolerance. Malian history was a major source of inspiration and held great importance for Keita. "In giving the name Mali to our young republic we have sworn before history to rehabilitate the moral values which formerly made the grandeur of Africa."[28] "Mali must be a continuation of the glorious Empire of the same name."[29] As part of a 1962 education reform, Keita promoted a vast enterprise aimed at the renewal of national culture. We can see his interest on this subject in the following quote:

> Fifty years of colonialism, one can not doubt, imprinted on our country a new face, isolated from its past and placed in bondage, destined to stifle all inclination of the resurgence of our traditions. The political and administrative institutions, economic and social structures, systems of teaching and education merged for the sole benefit of colonialism, a marked willingness to make the African irresponsible, incapable of initiative or inventive spirit, led certain of the colonized to adopt an attitude of passivity and submission vis-à-vis the colonizer and to accept the situation which he imposed. There were also some Africans who believed in the eternal nature of the colonial situation and acted as true dominators of their brothers. The same is certain of our compatriots who scorned our local traditions (written and oral), and profited by those of the conqueror; the intellectual colonialism

had begun an inexorable destruction of our national heritage and the corruption of our elites.

There is a disconcerting phenomena of collective depersonalization which will result in a total loss of our cultural values and of our civilization if the men, the Africans are not resolved to fight energetically against the spiritual death which menaces us all.[30]

On behalf of the Army, the head of an Army training school made an unequivocal commitment "to be the iron in the lance of the Socialist Revolution, to continue the radiance of Mali as it was in the days of Sundiata and Kan Kan Moussa." To which Keita responded,

I affirm with conviction the Malian Army and our security forces who are in the words of the Chief of State the most stable, the most engaged . . . and the most conscientious in the construction of our country and in the affirmation of moral values which made ancient Mali great and which permit the development and grandeur of the new Mali.[31]

Keita clearly equates national success with a return to traditional cultural values. But what is the content of those traditional values? For Keita and the US-RDA the emphasis was placed on communalism. This is, of course, consistent with the Marxist course of development that Keita was pursuing. Other elites had conflicting opinions while the village-based peasants seemed to stress the importance of local autonomy as a traditional value. Soon after independence, Keita began to extend and systematize the party apparatus. Hopkins claims that this was relatively successful.[32]

In the towns and the larger villages, self-government through the party apparatus came to take the place of self- government through the hierarchy of chiefs that the French had put in place, or through the play of a lineage system. . . . [T]he first step of the Malian government was to involve villagers and townspeople more closely in the new nation, and this meant establishing a series of new institutions of local government. People who felt themselves to be Malian, as Kitans did, considered that these institutions were Malian and thus legitimate. . . . Applying the principle of self-government at all levels, Kitans were as jealous of Mali's right to govern itself as they were of Kita's right to do so without interference from the national level.[33]

This conclusion seems essentially correct for large towns and the villages that surround them, but there are thousands of isolated communities in which the level of state penetration has never been significant. However, in areas where the party did establish new institutions of local government, they did not completely displace older institutions, social structures or basic political values. In contrast to Hopkins, I argue that political institutions in Mali have continued to be multi-layered. As in the case of education or medicine, Malians continue to use both traditional and modern methods in combination with the implicit belief that success in one method does not negate the need for the other.[34]

Keita used the imagery of the Empire of Mali and drew on civic community values as well as attempting to alter those values toward a "revolutionary" course. However, his initial popularity was ultimately lost when he began to forcefully intervene in local politics with party cadres that tried to replace the village council as the rural decision maker. And ultimately when he instituted a cultural revolution patterned on the cultural revolution of China.

Keita drew on political symbols from Mali's past to define his personal vision of Malian political culture throughout his tenure as president.[35] The electrician I met did the same as did the village chief of Kaba. This is common for Malian elites, and peasants alike although the meanings of the symbols themselves are often contested. This means the content of Mali's culture of politics is also not discrete but shifts and evolves with the needs of those who have the power to shape the discourse.

Despite great efforts by the military regime of Moussa Traoré and the socialist regime of Keita before him, the state has not been able to completely control the symbols of Malian political life. The symbols have a resilience and deep meaning that helps to shape a civic community in Mali supportive of democratic institutions. The rhythm of this civic community can be found in daily activities, occasional performance events and in national politics. It seems clear then that attention to the role of rhythm in public performance and oral history will enhance our basic understanding of political transitions in Africa. If rhythm plays a central role in almost all of Malian life then its role in political transitions may well provide a great deal of insight into the basic nature of these phenomena.

NOTES

Introduction

1. Cited in John Miller Chernoff, *African Rhythm and Sensibility: Aesthetics and Social Action in African Musical Idioms* (Chicago: University of Chicago Press, 1979), 23.

2. Ibid.

3. John Horton, "Time and Cool People," in *Rappin' and Stylin' Out,* ed. Thomas Kochman (Urbana: University of Illinois Press, 1972), 19.

4. Ibid.

5. Ben Sidran, *Black Talk* (New York, DaCapo, 1970), 7–8.

6. Raymond Williams, *The Long Revolution* (New York: Columbia University Press, 1961), 24–25.

7. Molefi Kete Asante, *The Afrocentric Idea* (Philadelphia: Temple University Press, 1987), 6.

8. Dona Marimba Richards, "The Implications of African American Spirituality," in *African Culture: The Rhythms of Unity,* ed. Molefi Kete Asante and Kariamu Welsh-Asante (Trenton, N.J.: Africa World Press, 1990), 220.

9. Kariamu Welsh-Asante, "The Aesthetic Conceptualization of *Nzuri,*" in *The African Aesthetic: Keeper of the Traditions,* ed. Kariamu Welsh-Asante (Westport, Conn.: Praeger, 1994), 12.

10. Carlton W. Molette and Barbara J. Molette, *Black Theatre: Premise and Presentation* (Bristol, Ind.: Wyndham Hall, 1986), 75.

11. Jon Michael Spencer, *Protest and Praise: Sacred Music of Black Religion* (Minneapolis, Minn.: Fortress Press, 1990), 141.

12. Ibid., 140.

13. Spencer, *The Rhythms of Black Folk: Race, Religion and Pan-Africanism* (Trenton, N.J.: Africa World Press, 1995), xv.

14. Ibid., xxiii-xxiv.

15. Chernoff, 37.

16. Zadia Ife, "The African Diasporan Ritual Mode," in *The African Aesthetic: Keeper of the Traditions,* ed. Kariamu Welsh-Asante (Westport, Conn.: Praeger, 1994), 35.

17. Welsh-Asante, "The Aesthetic Conceptualization of *Nzuri,*" 12.

18. See Welsh-Asante, ed., *The African Aesthetic: Keeper of the Traditions* (Westport, Conn.: Praeger, 1994).

Chapter One: A Rap on Rhythm

1. Regarding *nada* ("sound"), Hindu and Buddhist tantras hold that "the world shows itself, or is represented in us in the miniature, in the production of sound. The process of the production of sound is the epitome of the notion . . . of the cosmic process of creation." Shashi B. Dasgupta, *An Introduction to Tantric Buddhism* (Berkeley and London: Shambala, 1974), 60–61.

2. Rosalind Jeffries, "Black Hair Sculpture: An Art Historian's View," paper presented at the Contemporary Black American Braids symposium at the National Museum of

American History, Washington, D.C., November 1982.

3. Rupert Sheldrake introduced his thesis in *New Science of Life* (Los Angeles: J. P. Tarcher, 1981). See also his *The Rebirth of Nature* (New York: Bantam, 1992) and *Seven Experiments That Could Change The World: A Do-It-Yourself Guide to Revolutionary Science* (London: Fourth Estate, 1994).

4. Zora Neale Hurston, *Mules and Men* (Philadelphia: J. P. Lippincott, 1935), 229.

5. Writers Program, Virginia, *The Negro in Virginia* (New York: Hastings House, 1940), 93.

6. One of the points that John Miller Chernoff makes about the metronomic pulse is that we "begin to 'understand' African music by being able to maintain, in our minds or our bodies, an *additional* rhythm to the one we hear." John Miller Chernoff, *African Rhythm and African Sensibility: Aesthetics and Social Action in African Musical Idiom* (Chicago: University of Chicago Press, 1979), 49.

7. Writers Program, Virginia, 93.

8. Arnold Shaw, *The Jazz Age* (New York: Oxford University Press, 1987), 80.

9. Ibid., 82.

10. John Edward Hasse, *Beyond Category: The Life and Genius of Duke Ellington* (New York: Simon and Schuster, 1993), 189.

Chapter Two: Jazz Time and Our Time

1. Anthony Braxton, quoted in Valerie Wilmer, *As Serious As Your Life: The Story of the New Jazz* (1977; rpt., Westport, Conn.: Lawrence Hill and Co., 1980), 114.

2. Ronald M. Radano, *New Musical Figurations: Anthony Braxton's Cultural Critique* (Chicago: University of Chicago Press, 1993), 271; this issue is discussed on pp. 264–76.

3. Eric Nisenson, *Ascension: John Coltrane and His Quest* (New York: St. Martin's Press, 1993), 40ff.

4. John Coltrane, *My Favorite Things* (Atlantic 1361, 1960). Sound recording.

5. Nisenson, 94.

6. John S. Mbiti, *African Religions and Philosophy* (Garden City, N.Y.: Anchor Books, 1970), chapter 3, "The Concept of Time."

7. J. C. Thomas, *Chasin' the Trane: The Music and Mystique of John Coltrane* (New York: DaCapo, 1979), 133.

8. Ibid., 134.

9. John Coltrane, *Coltrane Live at the Village Vanguard Again!* (Impulse A-9124, 1966). Sound recording.

10. Thomas, 140.

11. Nisenson, 207.

12. Ibid.

13. Mircea Eliade, *Shamanism: Archaic Techniques of Ecstasy,* trans. Willard R. Trask (1951; rpt., Princeton: Princeton University Press, 1974).

14. Edward Strickland, "What Coltrane Wanted: The Legendary Saxophonist Forsook Lyricism for the Quest for Ecstasy," *Atlantic* (December 1987): 101, 102.

15. Cuthbert Ormond Simpkins, *Coltrane: A Biography* (New York: Herndon House, 1975), 206.

16. Nisenson, 205.

17. Nat Hentoff, liner notes to *John Coltrane—Meditations* (Impulse 9110, 1965). Sound recording.

18. Erich Neumann, "Art and Time," in *Man and Time: Papers from the Eranos Yearbooks,* ed. Joseph Campbell (1957; rpt., Princeton: Princeton University Press, 1983),

3–37. The quoted material is from pp. 24 and 32. This was originally presented at Eranos in 1951.

19. C. G. Jung, *Modern Man in Search of a Soul,* trans. W. S. Dell and Cary F. Baynes (New York: Harcourt Brace/Harvest Books, 1933), esp. chapter 8, "Psychology and Literature," pp. 152–72; see p. 172 for Jung's summary view of the *participation mystique.*

20. Neumann, 32.

21. Ibid., 29.

22. Bill Cole, *John Coltrane* (New York: Schirmer Books, 1976), 11.

23. Ibid.

24. Larry Birnbaum, "Art Ensemble of Chicago: Fifteeen Years of Great Black Music," *Downbeat* (May 3, 1979), 15–17, 39–42; quote on pp. 39–40; cf. John Litweiler, *The Freedom Principle: Jazz after 1958* (New York: Quill, 1984), chapter 8, "Chicago, Sound in Space," 172–99.

25. Stuart Broomer, "Early Art," *Coda* no. 256 (July–August 1994): 7–11; quote on p. 9.

26. Litweiler, 175.

27. Ekkehard Jost, *Free Jazz* (New York: DaCapo, 1981), 169ff.

28. Art Ensemble of Soweto/Art Ensemble of Chicago, with Amabutho Male Chorus, *America–South Africa* (DIW/Columbia 52954, 1991). Sound recording.

Chapter Three: Some Aesthetic Suggestions for a Working Theory of the "Undeniable Groove"

1. See Langston Hughes and Milton Meltzer, *Black Magic: A Pictorial History of the African-American in the Performing Arts* (New York: DaCapo, 1990), 11.

2. Henry Louis Gates, *The Signifying Monkey: A Theory of Afro-American Literary Criticism* (New York: Oxford University Press, 1988), xix-xx.

3. A. M. Jones, *African Rhythm* (London: International African Institute, 1965), 290–97.

4. John Miller Chernoff, *African Rhythm and African Sensibility: Aesthetics and Social Action in African Musical Idioms* (Chicago: University of Chicago Press, 1979), 155.

5. Ellen Conroy Kennedy, ed., *The Negritude Poets: An Anthology of Translations from the French* (New York: Thunder's Mouth Press, 1989), xxxi.

6. Gates, 3–4.

7. Robert Farris Thompson, *Flash of the Spirit: African and Afro-American Art and Philosophy* (New York: Random House, 1983), 19.

8. William C. Banfield, *What's the Right Note(G)?: Reflection or Projection: Insights into African American Artistic Expression* (Bloomington, Ind.: Tichnour Press, 1993), 71.

9. Queen Latifah, "Listen 2 Me," *Black Reign* (Motown Records 37463-6370, 1993). Sound recording.

10. Queen Latifah's descriptive handles as interpreted by William C. Banfield: (1) "in the house": the actual location where the party is taking place, i.e., a dance hall, house, or street; (2) "do'": door; (3) "diss": disrespect; (4) "whacked": goofy, not happening, and not flowing like Queen Latifah's lyrics are; and (5) "wreck it": dismantling another rapper's rap by boasting it down.

Chapter Four: Rhythm and Rhyme in Rap

1. Public Enemy, "Reggie Jax," *Fear of a Black Planet* (Def Jam CT-45413, 1990). Sound recording.

2. Jungle Brothers, "Doin' Our Own Thang," *Done by the Forces of Nature* (Warner Brothers 9-26072-4, 1989). Sound recording.

3. A Tribe Called Quest, "Rhythm (Devoted to the Art of Moving Butts)," *People's Instinctive Travels and the Paths of Rhythm* (Jive Records 1331-4-J, 1990). Sound recording.

4. MC Lyte, "Slave 2 the Rhythm," *Eyes on This* (Atlantic A4-91304, 1989). Sound recording.

5. Public Enemy, "Revolutionary Generation."

6. Salt-n-Pepa, "Let the Rhythm Run," *Colors* (Warner Brothers 9-25713-1, 1988). Sound recording.

7. Cornel West, "On Afro-American Popular Music: From Bebop to Rap," in his *Prophetic Fragments* (Grand Rapids, Mich.: Eerdmans, 1988), 186.

8. Kool Moe Dee, "Get the Picture," *Knowledge Is King* (Jive Records 1182-4-J, 1989). Sound recording.

9. Ibid., "I Go to Work."

10. Ibid., "I'm Hittin' Hard."

11. Ice Cream Tee, "To Be Continued," *Can't Hold Back* (Uni Records UNI-9, 1989). Sound recording.

12. MC Lyte, "Stop, Look, Listen."

13. Queen Latifah, "Come Into My House," *All Hail the Queen* (Tommy Boy Music TBC-1022, 1989). Sound recording.

14. Too Nice, "The Phantom of Hip Hop," *Cold Facts* (Arista Records A1-8583, 1989). Sound recording.

15. Carlton W. Molette and Barbara J. Molette, *Black Theatre: Premise and Presentation* (Bristol, Ind.: Wyndham Hall, 1986), 89.

16. Ibid., 88–89.

17. I emphasize here "commercialized rap" because the oral history of early rap and deejay music shows that rap music was indeed improvised on the spot with deejays and MC's commenting on the party they were attending and on their environment as it changed.

18. This point is also well taken by Tricia Rose in her article "Orality and Technology: Rap Music and Afro-American Cultural Resistance," *Popular Music and Society* 13.4 (Winter 1989): 40.

19. Madeline Slovenz, "'Rock the House': The Aesthetic Dimensions of Rap Music in New York City," *New York Folklore* 14.3–4 (1988): 159.

20. Melville J. Herskovits, *The Myth of the Negro Past* (Boston: Beacon, 1990), 265.

21. Dwight D. Andrews, "From Black to Blues," *Black Sacred Music: A Journal of Theomusicology* 6.1 (Spring 1992): 54–55.

22. Molefi Kete Asante, *The Afrocentric Idea* (Philadelphia: Temple University Press, 1987), 179.

23. Queen Latifah, "Come Into My House."

24. Kool Moe Dee, "I'm Hittin' Hard."

25. Philip M. Royster, "The Rapper as Shaman for a Band of Dancers of the Spirit: 'U Can't Touch This,'" *Black Sacred Music* 5.1 (Spring 1991): 65.

26. Ibid., 145–46.

27. Cited in Lawrence W. Levine, *Black Culture and Black Consciousness: Afro-American Folk Thought from Slavery to Freedom* (New York: Oxford University Press, 1977), 146.

28. Harry Oster, "The Blues as a Genre," in *Folklore Genres,* ed. Dan Ben-Amos (Austin: University of Texas Press, 1976), 62, 68.

29. Georgia Tom (Famous Hokum Boys), "Eagle Ridin' Papa," *Georgia Tom, 1929–1930* (Best of Blues BOB-18, [198-?]). Sound recording.

30. Naughty by Nature, "Yoke the Joker," *Naughty by Nature* (Tommy Boy Music TBCD-1044, 1991). Sound recording.

31. Molette and Molette, 82–83.

32. Public Enemy, "Fight the Power."

33. Naughty by Nature, "The Wickedest Man Alive."

34. Ibid., "Rhyme'll Shine On."

35. Ibid., "O. P. P."

36. Kool Moe Dee, "How Ya Like Me Now," *How Ya Like Me Now* (Jive Records 1079-4-J, 1987). Sound recording.

37. Yo-Yo, "Make Way for the Motherlode," *Make Way for the Motherlode* (East West Records America 7-91605-4, 1991). Sound recording.

38. Queen Latifah, "Dance for Me."

39. Above the Law, "Just Kickin' Lyrics," *Livin' Like Hustlers* (Ruthless Records ET-46041, 1990). Sound recording.

40. Cited in John Miller Chernoff, *African Rhythm and Sensibility: Aesthetics and Social Action in African Musical Idioms* (Chicago: University of Chicago Press, 1979), 23.

Chapter Five: The Music of Martin Luther King, Jr.

1. On the figures of speech, see Edward Corbett, *Classical Rhetoric for the Modern Student,* 2nd ed. (New York: Oxford University Press, 1971), 471–76. On alliteration see Martin Luther King, Jr., "I Have a Dream," in *Testament of Hope: The Essential Writings of Martin Luther King, Jr.,* ed. James Washington (San Francisco: Harper and Row, 1986), 219 (hereafter abbreviated as *Testament*).

2. King, "The Meaning of Hope" (sermon, 1967), Martin Luther King, Jr., Center for Nonviolent Social Action, Atlanta, Georgia (hereafter abbreviated MLK Center).

3. King, "Our God is Marching On," *Testament,* 230.

4. King, "Remaining Awake Through a Great Revolution" (speech, 1964), audio tape, Duke Divinity School Media Center.

5. The works of several scholars have been indispensable to my study of the musicality of King's preaching. Among them are Jon Michael Spencer, *Sacred Symphony: The Chanted Sermon of the Black Preacher* (New York: Greenwood Press, 1987), 1–16, and, perhaps more important, his personal conversations with me; William Turner, "The Musicality of Black Preaching: A Phenomenology" (unpublished manuscript); and Henry Mitchell, *Black Preaching* (Philadelphia: Lippincott, 1970); 162–89. A rich sourcebook on the language of black America is Geneva Smitherman, *Talkin and Testifyin* (Boston: Houghton Mifflin, 1977), 101–45.

6. Quoted in Gerald Davis, *I Got the Word In Me and I Can Sing It, You Know: A Study of the Performed African-American Sermon* (Philadelphia: University of Pennsylvania Press, 1985), epigraph.

7. Spencer, 4–5. On rhythm see Bruce Rosenberg, *Can These Bones Live? The Art of the American Folk Preacher,* rev. ed. (Urbana: University of Illinois Press, 1988), 71–72.

8. King, "Great . . . But" (sermon, 1967). Audio tape, MLK Center.

9. Herbert Marks, "On Prophetic Stammering," in *The Book and the Text: The Bible and Literary Theory,* ed. Regina M. Schwartz (Oxford: Basil Blackwell, 1990), 67. See also Mitchell, 176.

10. King, "Guidelines for a Constructive Church" (sermon, 1966), MLK Center.

11. King, "Some Things We Must Do" (sermon, 1957), quoted in Lucy Keele, "A Burkeian Analysis of the Rhetorical Strategies of Dr. Martin Luther King, Jr., 1955–1968," Ph.D. diss., University of Oregon, 1972, 165.

12. King, "A Knock at Midnight" (sermon, 1967 or 1968), audio tape, Duke Divinity School Media Center.

13. King, "Birmingham Negroes' Plea for Freedom" (speech, 1963), audio tape, MLK Center.

14. Smitherman, 134–37. See also Molefi Kete Asante, *The Afrocentric Idea* (Philadelphia: Temple University Press, 1987), 84–85.

15. Spencer, *Sacred Symphony,* 15–16. See also Gerald Davis's discussion of melisma, "the production of several notes around one syllable" (80). On the blue note see Janheinz Jahn, *Muntu: An Outline of Neo-African Culture,* trans. Marjorie Grene (London: Faber and Faber, 1958, 1961), 223.

16. King, "Great . . . But."

17. Conversations with Jon Michael Spencer.

18. King, "The Drum Major Instinct" (sermon, 1968), audio tape, MLK Center.

19. Smitherman, 104–13; Spencer, 5–8; Mitchell, 167–68.

20. Pat Watters, *Down to Now* (New York: Pantheon, 1971), 14.

21. See Mervyn A. Warren, *Black Preaching: Truth and Soul* (Washington, D.C.: University Press of America, 1977), 27–28.

22. Quoted in Charles V. Hamilton, *The Black Preacher in America* (New York: Morrow, 1972), 29.

23. This is James Cone's point in *Speaking the Truth: Ecumenism, Liberation, and Black Theology* (Grand Rapids, Mich.: Eerdmans, 1986), 27, 130.

24. Interview with Wyatt Tee Walker.

25. David L. Lewis, *King: A Critical Biography* (New York: Praeger, 1970), 394. For more on this discussion see Richard Lischer, *The Preacher King: Martin Luther King, Jr., and the Word that Moved America* (New York: Oxford University Press, 1995).

Chapter Six: Rhythm in Claude McKay's "Harlem Dancer"

1. These and subsequent lines from "Harlem Dancer" are taken from Dudley Randall, ed., *The Black Poets* (New York: Bantam, 1971), 59.

2. Throughout this analysis the word *rime* will be utilized to refer to meter arrangement; the word *rhyme* will be synonymous with the word *rhythm,* relative to shifts in tempo pertaining to language, music, and biology.

3. Quoted in Wayne F. Cooper, ed., *The Passions of Claude McKay* (New York: Schocken Books, 1973), 137.

4. David Levering Lewis, *When Harlem Was in Vogue* (New York: Oxford University Press, 1979), 30–32.

5. Quoted in Jervis Anderson, *This Was Harlem* (New York: Noonday Press, 1981), 74.

6. David A. Horowitz, Peter N. Carroll, and David D. Lee, *On the Edge: A History of Twentieth-Century America* (New York: West Publishing Co., 1990), 139.

7. Cary D. Wintz, *Black Culture and the Harlem Renaissance* (Houston: Rice University Press, 1989), 91.

8. Ibid.

Chapter Seven: Chanting Down Babylon

1. In this essay, I wish not to enumerate Rastafarian belief by numbered theses. In one important sense, this would be antithetical to the very dynamism of Rastafarianism, which, despite the "-ism," is far from monolithic. Here I want to give a brief account of the early development of this rich and varied religion and then explore specific beliefs in the poetry of the three writers I touch upon. Readers interested in learning systematically, however, may consult two of my earlier articles: "Rastafarianism: A Ministry for Social Change?" *Modern Churchman* n.s. 31, no. 3 (1989): 45–48; and "Poetic Liberation:

Rastafarianism, Poetry, and Social Change." *Modern Churchman* n.s. 34, no. 2 (1992): 16–21.

2. Louise Bennett, "Back to Africa," in *Black Youth, Rastafarianism, and the Identity Crisis in Britain,* ed. Len Garrison (London: ACER Project Publication, 1979), 8.

3. See Mervyn Morris, "Mikey Smith: Dub Poet," *Jamaican Journal* 18 (1985):42.

4. Ibid.

5. Ibid., 40.

6. Ibid., 45.

7. Ibid.

8. Ibid.

9. Ibid., 42. There is now a recording available: *Me Cyaan Believe It* (Island Records ILPS 9717, 1982).

10. Mutabaruka, *The First Poems* (Kingston: Paul Issa Publications, 1980), 26.

11. Ibid.

12. Ibid., 27.

13. Ibid., 25.

14. Ibid., 28.

15. Ibid.

16. See Middleton, "Rastafarianism: A Ministry for Social Change?" 45–48.

17. Mutabaruka, *The First Poems,* 28.

18. See Bob Marley, "Get Up Stand Up," *Legend: The Best of Bob Marley and the Wailers* (Island Records, 1984). Sound recording.

19. Mutabaruka, *The First Poems,* 62.

20. Benjamin Zephaniah, *The Dread Affair* (London: Arena Publications, 1985), 54.

21. Ibid., 55.

22. Ibid., 60.

23. Ibid., 61.

24. Ibid., 79.

25. Ibid., 81.

26. Ibid., 24, 25.

Chapter Eight: Rhythm as Modality and Discourse in *Daughters of the Dust*

1. Klaus de Albuquerque, "On *Daughters of the Dust*," *Reconstruction* 2 (1993): 123.

2. This quote and an interview with Dash were taken from Greg Tate, "Of Homegirl Goddesses and Geechee Women: The Afrocentric Cinema of Julie Dash," *Village Voice* (June 4, 1991): 78.

3. Ibid.

4. The term *Gullah* is used by Dash and other critics, but many Sea Island communities take offense and prefer to be called Sea Islanders.

5. Stanley Kauffmann, "Books and Arts: Stanley Kauffmann on Films," *New Republic* (February 10, 1992): 26.

6. Toni Bambara and bell hooks, *Daughters of the Dust* (New York: New York Press, 1992), xvi.

7. Ibid., 164.

8. Ibid.

9. de Albuquerque, "On *Daughters of the Dust*," 123.

10. Ibid., 125.

11. Ibid.

12. Quoted in Jahn Janheinz, *Muntu: African Cultures and the Western World* (New York: Grove Press, 1961), 164.

13. Ibid., 169.

14. Ibid., 164.

15. Trinh T. Minh-ha, "Grandma's Story," in her *Woman, Native, Other* (Bloomington: Indiana University Press, 1989), 121.

16. Mikhail Bakhtin, *The Dialogical Imagination: Four Essays by M. M. Bakhtin,* ed. Michael Holquist, trans. Caryl Emerson and Michael Holquist (Austin: University of Texas Press, 1981), 43.

17. Richard Rogers, "Rhythm and the Performance of Organization," *Text and Performance Quarterly* 14.3 (Summer 1994): 222–23.

18. Despite certain critics' assertions that the film is nonlinear, it clearly contains a sequential progression: first, the family members gather together from near and far; second, the family members then prepare for their journey; and third, the family members depart for their journey. Although there are flashbacks interspersed throughout the story, the overriding plot structure is not rearranged.

19. Rogers, 223.

20. Patricia Smith, "A Daughter's Tale," *Boston Globe* (March 15, 1992): B33.

21. Tate, 78.

22. Ibid.

23. Donna Britt, "Film Gets to the Coifed Roots of the African American Aesthetic," *Washington Post* (June 16, 1992): B1.

24. Eleanor Ringel, "A Dash of Poetry Inspires 'Daughters of the Dust,'" *Atlantic Constitution* (March 13, 1992): D1.

25. Barbara Myerhoff, "Life History among the Elderly: Performance, Visibility, and Re-membering," in *A Crack in the Mirror: Reflexive Perspectives in Anthropology,* ed. J. Ruby (Philadelphia: University of Pennsylvania Press, 1982), 103.

26. Victor Turner, *From Ritual to Theatre: The Human Seriousness of Play* (New York: Performing Arts Journal Publications, 1982), 149.

27. Ibid., 243.

28. Ibid., 16–24.

29. Ibid., 20.

30. Paul James Gee, "Literacy, Discourse, and Linguistics," *Journal of Education* 171 (1989): 6.

31. Bambara and hooks, 154.

32. This is the term Dash used in an interview to describe the moment when a people must leave their "homeplace" and move on.

33. Bambara and hooks, 157.

34. Ibid., 106.

Chapter Nine: Rhythms of Resistance

Author's note: This article is dedicated to the many people in South Africa who encouraged me to learn from and share in their freedom struggle. I am especially grateful to Paks Madikiza, currently of Ontario, Canada, who provided songs from the Pan Africanist Congress and translated most of the lyrics and colloquialisms in this essay from Xhosa, Zulu, and Sotho. Additional support was provided by E. Lizo Mazwai of the University of Transkei and Rev. Desmond Hoffmeister of the Baptist Convention of South Africa. The author is solely responsible for this paper's content and analysis.

1. According to 1991 census data, the most commonly spoken "mother tongues" in South Africa are Zulu (8.35 million), Xhosa (6.7 million), Afrikaans (5.75 million), and English (3.4 million). Other significant languages include Tswana, Sotho, Venda, Pedi,

and Tsonga. See Anton Harber and Barbara Ludman, *Weekly Mail and Guardian A-Z of South African Politics: The Essential Handbook* (London: Penguin, 1994), 285–86.

2. For theoretical discussions see Delores S. Williams, *Sisters in the Wilderness* (Maryknoll, N.Y.: Orbis Books, 1993); and Maxine Baca Zinn and Bonnie Thornton Dill, eds., *Women of Color in U.S. Society* (Philadelphia: Temple University Press, 1994).

3. Mary DeShazer, *A Poetics of Resistance: Women Writing in El Salvador, South Africa, and the United States* (Ann Arbor: University of Michigan Press, 1994), 2.

4. Quoted in Alec J. C. Pongweni, *Songs That Won the Liberation War* (Harare, Zimbabwe: College Press, 1982), iii.

5. Jonas Gwangwa and Fulco van Aurich, "The Melody of Freedom: A Reflection on Music," in *Culture in Another South Africa,* ed. Willem Campschreur and Joost Divendal (London: Zed Books, 1989), 147.

6. Mary Benson, *The African Patriots* (Chicago: Encyclopedia Britannica Press, 1963), 27.

7. Lovedale Sol-fa leaflet no. 17 (South Africa: Lovedale Press, n.d.). For the Negro Spirituals see W. E. B. DuBois, *The Souls of Black Folk* (Greenwich, Conn.: Fawcett, 1961); and Alain Locke, ed., *The New Negro* (New York: Atheneum, 1980).

8. In 1994 Zimbabwe adopted a new national anthem, based on an indigenous composition, entitled "Bless Zimbabwe," partly to strengthen national unity but also to establish a national identity distinct from that of the new South Africa.

9. David Chidester, *Shots in the Streets: Violence and Religion in South Africa* (Boston: Beacon Press, 1991), 117.

10. Ibid., 118–19.

11. Cited in Peter Magubane and Carol Lazar, *Women of South Africa: Their Fight for Freedom* (Boston: Little, Brown, 1993), 37.

12. For a detailed discussion of women's resistance to the pass laws see Julia C. Wells, *We Now Demand! The History of Women's Resistance to Pass Laws in South Africa* (Johannesburg: Witswatersrand University Press, 1993).

13. Magubane and Lazar, 39.

14. The National Party government eventually turned the tribal reserves into ten "bantustans," or "homelands," which were in turn accorded counterfeit "independent nation" status. The homelands were formally reincorporated into the nation in 1994.

15. Fatima Meer, *Higher than Hope: The Authorized Biography of Nelson Mandela* (New York: Harper and Row, 1990), 139.

16. Sobukwe was jailed for his leadership role in the Sharpeville protests.

17. Ibid., 147.

18. Sipho Buthelezi, "The Emergence of Black Consciousness: An Historical Appraisal," in Barney Pityana et al., eds., *Bounds of Possibility: The Legacy of Steve Biko and Black Consciousness* (Cape Town: David Philip Publishers, 1991), 112.

19. Corbin Seavers, *Apartheid: The Untold Story* (Hampton, Va.: United Brothers and Sisters, 1992), 23.

20. *Azania News* (Central Committee of the PAC of Azania, 1990), vol. 26.

21. Ibid.

22. Chidester, *Shots in the Dark,* 121, 192–93 n.16.

23. An illuminating discussion of the need to similarly liberate sacred song in the African American experience is found in Jon Michael Spencer, *Sing a New Song: Liberating Black Hymnody* (Minneapolis: Fortress Press, 1995).

24. Sheridan Johns and R. Hunt Davis, Jr., eds., *Mandela, Tambo, and the African National Congress: The Struggle Against Apartheid, 1948–1990* (Oxford: Oxford University Press, 1991), 138.

25. Howard Barrell, *MK: The ANC's Armed Struggle* (London: Penguin Books, 1990), 4.

26. Mandela was arrested at a roadblock in Natal in August 1962 after an American CIA agent apparently tipped off the South African police. Ibid., 13.

27. Julie Frederikse, *The Unbreakable Thread: Non-Racialism in South Africa* (Johannesburg: Raven Press, 1990), 246.

28. Additional influences came from the African American freedom struggle, African independence movements, Marxist- Leninism, and others of the two-thirds world. African American kindred spirits include Stokely Carmichael, Huey P. Newton, H. Rap Brown, Angela Davis, Eldridge Cleaver, Martin Luther King, Jr., Malcolm X, Shirley Chisholm, James Cone, Vincent Harding, C. Eric Lincoln, and Lerone Bennett. Other philosophical witnesses include Paulo Freire (Brazil), Mao Tse-tung (China), Frantz Fanon (Martinique-Algeria), Aime' Cesaire (Caribbean), Leopold Sedar Senghor (Senegal), Ernesto "Che" Guevara (Cuba), and even Antonio Gramsci (Italy). See Pityana et al, eds., *Bounds of Possibility*, and Themba Sono, *Reflections on the Origins of Black Consciousness in South Africa* (Pretoria: Human Sciences Research Council, 1993).

29. Cosmo Pieterse, "A Reflection on South African Poetry," in Campschreur and Divendal, *Culture in Another South Africa,* 112.

30. N. Barney Pityana, "The Legacy of Steve Biko," in Pityana et al., eds., *Bounds of Possibility,* 255.

31. Despite the cultural ideals of the BCM, traditional gender-based disparities between men and women remained. See Mamphela Ramphele, "The Dynamics of Gender within Black Consciousness Organisations: A Personal View," in Pityana et al., eds., *Bounds of Possibility,* 217.

32. See Stephen Ellis and Tsepo Sechaba, *Comrades Against Apartheid* (Bloomington: Indiana University Press, 1992), 84; and Barrell, 33.

33. Jacklyn Cock, *Women and War in South Africa* (Cleveland: Pilgrim Press, 1993), 221.

34. Ibid., 222, 231–35.

35. Adelaide Tambo, ed., *Oliver Tambo Speaks* (London: Heinemann Educational Books, 1987), 128.

36. Ian Kerkhof, "Music and Censorship in South Africa," *Rixaka: Cultural Journal of the African National Congress* 2 (1986): 28.

37. Both songs are taken from the compilation recording *Radio Freedom* (Rounder Records, 1985).

38. Steve Clark, ed., *Nelson Mandela Speaks: Forging a Democratic, Nonracial South Africa* (New York: Pathfinder Press, 1993), 23.

39. Brenda Fasse, a popular singer in South Africa, recorded a song about Mandela entitled "Black President" in 1990.

40. Diana E. H. Russell, *Lives of Courage: Women for a New South Africa* (New York: Basic Books, 1989), 340.

41. Cock, 47.

42. For a more critical view of the ANC Women's League see Frene Ginwala, "Women and the Elephant: The Need to Redress Gender Oppression," *Putting Women on the Agenda,* ed. Susan Bazilla (Johannesburg: Raven Press, 1991), 62–74.

43. Clark, 48–52.

44. Mzwakhe, *Unbroken Spirit* (Shifty Records, 1989). Sound recording.

45. 200 IQ, *The Hour for Democracy,* commissioned by the Institute for Contextual Theology, Johannesburg, 1994.

46. Chidester, 167.

47. Heribert Adams and Kogila Moodley, *The Negotiated Revolution: Society in Post-Apartheid South Africa* (Johannesburg: Jonathan Ball Publishers, 1993), 129.

48. Sipho "Hotstix" Mabuse, "Ha A Yo," from the ANC compilation recording *Sekunjalo—Bread and Roses* (EMI Music, 1994).

Chapter Ten: The Rhythm of Everyday Politics

Author's note: I wish to express appreciation to Dr. Catharine Newbury, the Social Science Research Council, and especially to Heidi Hemming and Colin Souleymane Smith.

1. Elsewhere I call these long-term patterns of governance "civic community." See Zeric Kay Smith, "Democracy and Civic Community in Mali," master's thesis, University of North Carolina, 1993.

2. Very little current social science literature on political transitions in Africa takes seriously the call for greater interdisciplinarity. A recent conference co-sponsored by the Social Science Research Council and the University of North Carolina at Chapel Hill is a notable exception. See Lisa Richey and Zeric Kay Smith, "Report, Summary, and Analysis of Political Transitions in Africa" (Social Science Research Council, 1994). Hale recently wrote that to find the answers to many "mysteries, [one] must draw on the expertise of the linguistic anthropologist, the ethnologist, the historian, the Arabist, the sociologist and representatives of many other specialties. . . . We need, then, to build new bridges across disciplines if we are to understand the Sahel. When the texts that fascinate scholars in literature, history, anthropology, or folklore are viewed in a comparative perspective and analyzed with information from recent work by archaeologists, climatologists, and other scientists, they promise to give us a clearer contemporary portrait of the peoples in the Sahel." Thomas A. Hale, *Scribe, Griot, and Novelist: Narrative Interpreters of the Songhay Empire followed by the Epic of Askia Mohammed Recounted by Nouhou Malio* (Gainesville: University of Florida Press/Center for African Studies, 1990), 31. I would add political science to his list of academic fields that could benefit from greater interdisciplinarity.

3. Patrick R. McNaughton, *The Mande Blacksmiths: Knowledge, Power, and Art in West Africa,* Traditional Arts of Africa series, eds. Paula Ben-Amos, Roy Sieber, and Robert Farris Thompson (Bloomington: Indiana University Press, 1988), 24.

4. Ibid., 25.

5. Ibid.

6. See especially Mary Jo Arnoldi, *Playing with Time: Art and Performance in Central Mali* (Bloomington: Indiana University Press, 1995); and Mary Jo Arnoldi, "Tradition and Innovation in the Sogobo Masquerade Theater in Segou," paper presented at the International Mande Studies Association Conference, Bamako, Mali, 1992; also Alastair Guild, "The Puppet Master," *Focus on Africa* 3, no. 2 (April–June 1992): 36–40; Nicholas S. Hopkins, "*Le Théâtre Moderne au Mali,*" *Presence Africaine* 53 (1965): 162–93; Pascal James Imperato, "The Depiction of Beautiful Women in Malian Youth Association Masquerades," *African Arts* (January 1994): 58–96; Claude Meillassoux, "The 'Koteba' of Bamako," *Presence Africaine* 24, no. 52 (1964): 28–62; Cornelia Panazacchi, "The Livelihoods of Traditional Griots in Modern Senegal," *Africa* 64, no. 2 (1994): 191–210; Paul Stoller, "Ethnographies as Texts/Ethnographers as Griots," *American Ethnologist* 21, no. 2 (1994): 353–66; and John W. Nunley, *Moving with the Face of the Devil: Art and Politics in Urban West Africa.* (Urbana: University of Illinois Press, 1987).

7. Deborah Heath, "The Politics of Appropriateness and Appropriation: Recontextualizing Women's Dance in Urban Senegal," *American Ethnologist* 21, no. 1 (1994): 90.

8. Ibid., 88.

9. *Le pouvoir se mange entire* ("power is eaten whole"). This saying from south eastern Zaire serves as the centerpiece and starting point for Fabian's exploration of issues of performance and politics. Johannes Fabian, *Power and Performance: Ethnographic Explorations through Proverbial Wisdom and Theatre in Shaba, Zaire* (Madison: University of Wisconsin Press, 1990).

10. On this point see James C. Scott, *Weapons of the Weak: Everyday Forms of Peasant Resistance* (New Haven: Yale University Press, 1985); and James C. Scott, *Domination and the Arts of Resistance: Hidden Transcripts* (New Haven: Yale University Press, 1990).

11. I argue in Smith 1993 that the culture of politics in Mali is not hostile to democracy, and that the state, in the role of local bureaucrats or on a national level, can either hinder or foster the development of a national political culture that is hospitable to democratic institutions. I also stress that political culture is not any more immutable than other cultural practices, and the meaning and content of terms such as *democracy* and *multiparty* are often contested.

12. Arnoldi, *Playing with Time,* and Arnoldi, "Tradition and Innovation," 1992.

13. Ibid.

14. I follow Brenner here by using *le pouvoir* to refer to the Malian state. This is common usage in Mali and reveals a particular vision of the state on the part of Malians. See Louis Brenner, "Youth as Political Actors in Mali," in *Political Transitions in Africa: Expanding Political Space,* eds. Catharine Newbury, Pearl T. Robinson, and Mamadou Diop, forthcoming.

15. Theses categories are justified and explained in depth in Smith 1993, see especially pp. 24–26.

16. The term *culture of politics* has been adopted by Robinson to "signal a departure from the conventional treatment of political culture"; Pearl T. Robinson, "Regime Change and the Culture of Politics," *African Studies Review* 37, no. 1 (April 1994): 63n.4. For conventional treatments of political culture see Gabriel A. Almond and Sidney Verba, *The Civic Culture* (Boston: Little, Brown, 1965); Ronald Inglehart, "The Renaissance of Political Culture," *American Political Science Review* 82, no. 4 (December 1988): 1203–30; and, questioning some of the former methods, Edward N. Muller and Mitchell A. Seligson, "Civic Culture and Democracy: The Question of Causal Relationship," *American Political Science Review* 88, no. 3 (September 1994): 635–52. For an extensive review of literature and critique of the concept of political culture see Smith 1993, 13–24. I follow Robinson in taking an analytical approach to these questions, which focuses on qualitative research methods.

17. Interview with Boubacar Traoré, May 1993. Notes in possession of author. This interview was rather remarkable as Traoré dramatically echoed my own hypothesis about the role of political symbols in modern Malian politics. The interview was conducted in French and I transcribed it directly into English in my field log. The quotations thus represent a very close approximation of Traoré's words. He was not aware of the nature of my research or my previous work, only that I was studying politics in Mali.

18. For examples of the Sundiata epic, see Djibril Tamsir Niane, *Soundjata; Ou, L'Epopie Mandingue* (Paris: Presence Africaine, 1971); Gordon Innes, *Sunjata: Three Mandinka Versions* (London: School of Oriental and African Studies, University of London, 1974); John William Johnson, *The Epic of Son-Jara: A West African Tradition,* trans. John William Johnson; text by Fa-Digi Sisòkò (Bloomington: Indiana University Press, 1986); and John William Johnson, *The Epic of Son-Jara: A West African Tradition;* notes, translation, and new introduction by John William Johnson, text by Fa-Digi Sisòkò (Bloomington: Indiana University Press, 1992).

19. Interview with Traoré.

20. Cheick Oumar Diarrah, *Le Mali de Modibo Keita* (Paris: Éditions L'Harmattan, 1986), 9. All documents in French are translated by the author.

21. Ibid., 223.

22. Ibid., 221.

23. Frank George Snyder, *One-Party Government in Mali: Transition Toward Control* (New Haven: Yale University Press, 1965), 24–25; and Catherine Coquery-Vidrovitch, *Africa: Endurance and Change South of the Sahara* (Berkeley: University of California Press, 1988), 276.

24. Hopkins, 168.

25. Meillassoux, 30.

26. Ibid., 61.

27. Ibid., 56.

28. Ruth Schachter Morgenthau, *Political Parties in French-Speaking West Africa* (Oxford: Clarendon Press, 1964), 300.

29. Diarrah, 182.

30. Ibid., 88–89.

31. Bintou Sanankoua, *La Chute de Modibo Keita* (Paris: Editions Chaka, 1990), 81–82.

32. Hopkins did his field work in the large eastern town of Kita and in a few surrounding villages. Kitans are residents of Kita.

33. Nicholas S. Hopkins, *Popular Government in an African Town: Kita, Mali* (Chicago: University of Chicago Press, 1972), 17.

34. In the case of health care, "Mali's national health policy . . . supports *two* medicines—traditional and biomedical and modern medicine does not, nor need it totally displace traditional healing practice." Kathleen Iverin Slobin, "Family Mediation of Health Care in an African Community (Mali)" (Ph.D. diss., University of California at San Francisco, 1991), 300. As for education, parents in Mali often send their children to Koranic school and public schools. In the village, attendance at a public school would be completely compatible with involvement in age-group activities structured around traditional education in village history and culture.

35. For a more complete evaluation of Keita's use of these cultural symbols see Smith 1993, 42–57.

SELECTED BIBLIOGRAPHY

Asante, Kariamu Welsh. "Commonalities in African Dance: An Aesthetic Foundation." In *African Culture: The Rhythms of Unity*, ed. Molefi Kete Asante and Kariamu Welsh Asante, 71–82. Trenton, N.J.: Africa World Press, 1990.

Asante, Molefi Kete. *The Afrocentric Idea*. Philadelphia: Temple University Press, 1987.

Baraka, Amiri (LeRoi Jones). *Blues People: The Negro Experience in White America and the Music That Developed from It*. New York: Morrow, 1963.

Barrett, Leonard. *Soul Force*. Garden City, N.Y.: Doubleday, 1974.

Bayer, Raymond. "The Essence of Rhythm." In *Reflections on Art: A Source Book of Writings by Artists, Critics, and Philosophers*, ed. Suzanne K. Langer. Baltimore: Johns Hopkins University Press, 1958.

Chernoff, John Miller. *African Rhythm and African Sensibility: Aesthetics and Social Action in African Musical Idioms*. Chicago: University of Chicago Press, 1979.

Cooper, Grosvenor W., and Leonard B. Meyer. *The Rhythmic Structure of Music*. Chicago: University of Chicago Press, 1963.

Courlander, Harold. *Negro Folk Music, U.S.A.* New York: Columbia University Press, 1963.

Dett, R. Nathaniel. "The Authenticity of the Spiritual." *Black Sacred Music: A Journal of Theomusicology* 5.2 (Fall 1991): 108–13.

———. "Negro Music." *Black Sacred Music: A Journal of Theomusicology* 5.2 (Fall 1991): 120–29.

Fanon, Frantz. *Black Skin, White Masks*. New York: Grove Press, 1967.

Gayle, Addison, ed. *The Black Aesthetic*. Garden City, N.Y.: Anchor Books, 1972.

Handy, W. C. *Blues: An Anthology*. New York: Albert and Charles Boni, 1926.

Harrison, Paul Carter. *The Drama of Nommo*. New York: Grove Press, 1972.

Herskovits, Melville J. *The Myth of the Negro Past*. Boston: Beacon Press, 1958.

Horton, John. "Time and Cool People." In *Rappin' and Stylin' Out: Communication in Urban Black America*, ed. Thomas Kochman, 19–31. Urbana: University of Illinois Press, 1972.

Hurston, Zora Neale. *The Sanctified Church*. Berkeley: Turtle Island Press, 1981.

Ife, Zadia. "The African Diasporan Ritual Mode." In *The African Aesthetic: Keeper of the Traditions*, ed. Kariamu Welsh-Asante, 31–51. Westport, Conn.: Praeger, 1994.

Jahn, Janheinz. *Muntu: The New African Culture*. New York: Grove Press, 1961.

James, Willis Laurence. *Stars in De Elements: A Study of Negro Folk Music*. Edited by Jon Michael Spencer. Special issue, *Black Sacred Music: A Journal of Theomusicology* 9 (1995).

Johnson, James Weldon. *Black Manhattan*. New York: Alfred A. Knopf, 1930.

Locke, Alain. *The Negro and His Music*. Washington, D.C.: Associates in Negro Folk Education, 1936.

Mbiti, John. *Introduction to African Religion*. Portsmouth, N.H.: Heinemann Educational Books, 1975.

Merriam, Alan P. "African Music." In *Continuity and Change in African Cultures*, ed. William R. Bascom and Melville J. Herskovits. Chicago: University of Chicago Press, 1959.

Molette, Carlton W., and Barbara J. Molette. *Black Theatre: Premise and Presentation*. Bristol, Ind.: Wyndham Hall, 1986.

Myers, Charles S. "A Study of Rhythm in Primitive Music." *British Journal of Psychology* 1 (1905): 397–406.

Nketia, J. H. Kwabena. "History and Organization of Music in West Africa." In *Essays on Music and History in Africa,* ed. Klaus P. Wachsmann. Evanston: Northwestern University Press, 1971.

Oderigo, Nestor R. Ortiz. "Negro Rhythm in the Americas." *African Music* 1.3 (1956): 68–69.

Odum, Howard W., and Guy B. Johnson. *The Negro and His Songs*. Hatboro, Penn.: Folklore Associates, 1964.

Parrish, Lydia. *Slave Songs of the Georgia Sea Islands*. New York: Creative Age Press, 1942.

Pasteur, Ivory, and Alfred Toldson. *Roots of Soul*. Garden City, N.Y.: Doubleday, 1982.

Pennington, Dorothy L. "Time in African Culture." In *African Culture: The Rhythms of Unity,* ed. Molefi Kete Asante and Kariamu Welsh Asante, 123–40. Trenton, N.J.: Africa World Press, 1990.

Radocy, Rudolf E., and J. David Boyle. *Psychological Foundations of Musical Behavior.* Springfield, Ill.: Charles C. Thomas, 1979.

Richards, Dona Marimba. "The Implications of African American Spirituality." In *African Culture: The Rhythms of Unity,* ed. Molefi Kete Asante and Kariamu Welsh Asante, 207–31. Trenton, N.J.: Africa World Press, 1990.

Sidran, Ben. *Black Talk*. New York: DaCapo, 1970.

Southern, Eileen. *The Music of Black Americans*. New York: Norton, 1983.

Spencer, Jon Michael. *Protest and Praise: Sacred Music of Black Religion*. Minneapolis, Minn.: Fortress Press, 1990.

———. "Rhythm in Black Religion of the African Diaspora." *Journal of Religious Thought* 44.2 (Winter–Spring 1988): 67–82.

———. *The Rhythms of Black Folk: Race, Religion, and Pan- Africanism*. Trenton, N.J.: Africa World Press, 1995.

Walton, Ortiz. *Music: Black, White, and Blue: A Sociological Survey of the Use and Misuse of Afro-American Music*. New York: Morrow, 1972.

Waterman, Richard Alan. "'Hot' Rhythm in Negro Music." *Journal of the American Musicological Society* 1 (Spring 1948): 24–37.

Welsh-Asante, Kariamu. "The Aesthetic Conceptualization of *Nzuri*." In *The African Aesthetic: Keeper of the Traditions,* ed. Kariamu Welsh-Asante, 1–20. Westport, Conn.: Praeger, 1994.

Welsh-Asante, Kariamu, ed. *The African Aesthetic: Keeper of the Traditions*. Westport, Conn.: Praeger, 1994.

Williams, Raymond. *The Long Revolution*. New York: Columbia University Press, 1961.

Wilson, Olly. "The Significance of the Relationship between Afro-American Music and West African Music." *Black Perspective of Music* 2.1 (Spring 1974): 3–20.

NOTES ON CONTRIBUTORS

William C. Banfield is an endowed chair in fine arts and humanities in the Department of Music at the University of St. Thomas. He received his doctorate in composition from the University of Michigan. A prolific composer, Dr. Banfield has written more than two hundred jazz, popular, gospel, and symphonic works. He is the author of *What's the Right Note (G)? Reflection or Projection: Insights into African American Artistic Expression* (1993).

Juliette Bowles is the editor of the *International Review of African American Art*. She is the scriptwriter of *Stories of Illumination and Growth: John Biggers and the Hampton Murals* (1993 Emmy Award nominee) and the award-winning PBS series *Juba*. Her articles have appeared in newspapers and journals. She received an M.A. in American studies from the College of William and Mary and an M.S. in television/radio/film from Syracuse University. Bowles has also worked as a visual artist.

Ronald Dorris Ronald Dorris is an associate professor of English and African American studies and is also the director of African American Studies at Xavier University of Louisiana. He received his Ph.D. in American studies from Emory University. Dorris is the author of *Race: Jean Toomer's Swan Song* (1997) and has contributed to *Perspectives of Black Popular Culture* (1990). In addition, his publications have appeared in *Black Sacred Music: A Journal of Theomusicology, Western Journal of Black Studies, Western Humanities Review, American Poetry Anthology, Griot, Proteus, McNeese Review, Louisiana English Journal,* and *Quarterly West*.

Mark S. Harvey is a lecturer in music at the Massachusetts Institute of Technology, where he teaches courses in jazz, American music, and other subjects. He is the music director and principal composer for the Aardvark Jazz Orchestra with which he has recorded four CDS of his original compositions. He has received awards from ASCAP and the *Meet the Composer*/Lila Wallace-Reader's Digest Commissioning Program. His articles on music, religion, and culture have appeared in *Black Sacred Music: A Journal of Theomusicology, Soundings, Religion and Intellectual Life, Theology Today,* and *Christian Century* and in the anthologies *Jazz in Mind* (1991) and *American Civilization* (1974). Harvey received his Ph.D. from Boston University Graduate School, Division of Theological and Religious Studies. He is a United Methodist minister.

Richard Lischer is a professor of homiletics in the Divinity School of Duke University. His books include *Marx and Teilhard: Two Ways to the New Humanity*

(1979), *A Theology of Preaching: The Dynamics of the Gospel* (1981), *Speaking of Jesus* (1982), *Theories of Preaching* (1987), and, his most recent work, *The Preacher King: Martin Luther King, Jr., and the Word That Moved America* (1995). He served as a parish pastor for nine years and has lectured at seminaries and universities in the United States, Canada, Norway, Zimbabwe, and Germany. Lischer received his Ph.D. in systematic theology from the University of London.

D. Soyini Madison is an associate professor of performance studies in the Department of Communication Studies and the associate director of the Institute of African American Research at the University of North Carolina at Chapel Hill. She received her Ph.D. from Northwestern University in Performance Studies. She is editor of *The Woman That I Am: The Literature and Culture of Contemporary Women of Color* (1994) and has contributed to *From Mouse to Mermaid: The Politics of Film, Gender, and Culture* (1995), *Exceptional Spaces: Essays in Performance and History* (1998), and *The Future of Performance Studies: Vision and Revision* (1998). Her articles have appeared in *Communication and Education, Text and Performance Quarterly,* and *Black Sacred Music: A Journal of Theomusicology.*

Darren J. N. Middleton Darren J. N. Middleton is an assistant professor of religion and culture at Texas Christian University. He received his Ph.D. from the Centre for the Study of Literature and Theology at the University of Glasgow, Scotland.

Middleton is the author of the forthcoming *Novel Theology: Kazantzakis's Encounter with Whiteheadian Process Theism* and co-editor of *God's Struggler: Religion in the Writings of Nikos Kazantzakis* (1996). He has also contributed to the *Journal of Modern Greek Studies, Process Studies,Modern Churchman,* and *Theology Themes.*

Angela M. S. Nelson is an assistant professor in the Department of Popular Culture and director of the Center for Popular Culture Studies at Bowling Green State University, where she received her Ph.D. in American culture studies. She has taught classes in popular culture, ethnic studies, music, and television. She has contributed to *Popular Culture: An Introductory Text* (1992), *Generations: Academic Feminists in Diaglogue* (1997), and the forthcoming *Signature Songs and Rhythms: Cultural and Physiological Aspects of African-American Music,* as well as *Black Sacred Music: A Journal of Theomusicology* and *Christian History.*

Alton B. Pollard III is director of Black Church Studies and an associate professor of religion and culture in the Candler School of Theology at Emory University. He received his Ph.D. in religion at Duke University. Pollard is the author of *Mysticism and Social Change: The Social Witness of Howard Thurman* (1992), and has contributed to *The Human Search: Howard Thurman and the Quest for Freedom* (1992), *Lure and Loathing: Essays on Race, Identity, and Assimilation* (1993), and *Redeeming Men: Essays on Men, Masculinity, and Religion* (1996). His articles have appeared in *Theology Today, Africa Today, Journal of*

Religious Thought, and *Black Sacred Music: A Journal of Theomusicology,* for which he served as associate editor.

Zeric Kay Smith is a visiting assistant professor and assistant director of the African Studies Program in the Department of Government and International Studies at the University of South Carolina. He completed his doctorate in political science at the University of North Carolina at Chapel Hill, where he has taught in the Departments of Political Science and African Studies Curriculum. Smith was the recipient of a 1995–96 Fulbright Scholarship and has contributed to *Black Sacred Music: A Journal of Theomusicology* and *Review of African Political Economy.*

INDEX